Presented to
St. Joseph's College
by the Author
Wm. J. Castleman
April 26, 1983

EX LIBRIS

SAINT JOSEPH'S COLLEGE
RENSSELAER INDIANA

GIFT FROM
AUTHOR

Beauty and the Mission of the Teacher

ALSO BY WILLIAM J. CASTLEMAN

On This Foundation: A Biography of the Early Life of Samuel Guy Inman, 1877-1904 (Vol. I)

Samuel Guy Inman: 1905-1916 (Vol. II)

Beauty and the Mission of the Teacher

The Life of Gabriela Mistral of Chile—
Teacher, Poetess, Friend of the Helpless,
Nobel Laureate

WILLIAM J. CASTLEMAN

AN EXPOSITION-UNIVERSITY BOOK

Exposition Press   Smithtown, New York

The poetry and prose works of Gabriela Mistral that appear in this volume are the author's translations or translations by Alice Stone Blackwell from *Some Spanish-American Poets* (New York, London: D. Appleton & Co., 1930).

FIRST EDITION

© 1982 by William J. Castleman

All rights reserved. No part of this book may be reproduced, in whole or in part, in any form or by any means, electronic or mechanical, including photocopying, recording, or by any information storage and retrieval system, without permission in writing from the publisher. Address inquiries to Exposition Press, Inc., 325 Rabro Drive, Smithtown, NY 11787-0817.

Library of Congress Catalog Card Number: 81-90674

ISBN 0-682-49853-X

Printed in the United States of America

To the thousands of teachers and workers with children and young people, as they strive to bring meaning and beauty into the lives of those with whom they work

Contents

	Preface	xi
1	THE EARLY YEARS	1
	Jerónimo	1
	Petronila	2
	A Daughter Is Born	2
	Marital Discord	3
	Emelina	4
	Monte Grande	5
	Childhood Dreams	6
	Vicuña	7
	La Serena	8
	Grandmother and the Bible	8
	A Love of Learning	9
2	EMERGING POETESS AND TEACHER	10
	Early Writings and First Jobs	10
	La Cantara	11
	Romance and Tragedy	12
	Secondary School Teacher	13
	Los Andes	15
3	GROWING RECOGNITION	17
	An Appeal to Rubén Darío	17
	Los Juegos Flores (The Floral Games)	20
	The Pseudonym	21
	Increased Recognition Within and Outside Chile	22
	Disappointment in Love	26

4 Flight to Forget — 30
- Patagonia — 30
- Temuco — 32
- Santiago and Liceo Number Six — 32

5 A New Career, Another Country — 34
- Invitation to Mexico — 34
- Palma Guillén — 35
- Gabriela in Mexico — 37
- *Desolación* — 38
- Gabriela and Guy Inman — 41
- *La Nueva Democracia* — 42
- A Champion of Women — 44
- Aroused Critics — 44

6 Life Abroad and Further Recognition — 46
- Visits to the United States and Europe — 46
- *Ternura* — 47
- Montivideo Conference — 49
- France — 53
- Spain — 55
- League of Nations — 56
- Juan Miguel — 57
- Alice Stone Blackwell — 58

7 Turning Points — 66
- Death of Petronila — 66
- A Spokeswoman for Latin America — 67
- Gabriela's Prose — 67
- United States—1930 — 68
- Puerto Rico and Central America — 69
- Back to Europe and Consular Service — 70
- Puerto Rico Again — 70
- Spain Again — 71
- Consul for Life — 72
- Chilean Follore Project — 73
- *Tala* — 75

Contents

8	THE NOBEL PRIZE	78
	Cuba	78
	A Consul's Life	78
	Two Tragedies	80
	Gabriela's Health	83
	The Nobel Prize	83
	European Visit	87
	Doris Dana	88
	White House Reception	88
	United Nations Delegate	89
9	FAILING HEALTH	90
	California	90
	Mexico Revisited	91
	More Travel	92
	Return to Chile	93
	Return to the United States	96
	Lagar	96
	"Poema de Chile"	98
	The Perfectionist	99
10	THE FINAL YEARS	100
	Universal Declaration of Human Rights	100
	Marie-Lise Gazarian-Gautier	101
	The Last Year	102
	Final Illness and Death	103
	Observance in Chile	106
	Universal Recognition	107
	Doris Dana's Mission	110
	EPILOGUE	111
	Notes	112
	Bibliography	115

Preface

"You shall love beauty," wrote Gabriela Mistral, "for it is the shadow of God over the universe."

What is beauty? Is it something that can be perceived by the senses? Can you see it, hear it, smell it? Is it something one can taste or touch? Does it require especially refined senses to fully apprehend its nature? Is beauty fleeting, passing in a moment like the breath of a summer breeze that may quickly die away? Or does it have the stability that causes it as a quality to linger on?

Much of Gabriela's ideal of beauty may be seen in her dedication to the task of teaching children as we look at a portion of her "Teacher's Prayer."

> Let me be more mother than the mother herself in my love and defense of the child who is not flesh of my flesh. Help me to make one of my children my most perfect poem, and leave within him or her my most melodious melody for that day when my own lips no longer sing.

1

The Early Years

JERÓNIMO

Jerónimo Godoy Villanueva, Gabriela Mistral's father, grew up in the northern part of Chile in a province noted for its legends, mines, and revolutions. In his youth, Jerónimo studied in the seminary at La Serena. His mother, a devoutly religious woman, had hoped to see her son become a priest; her two daughters had already entered convents.

To his mother's disappointment, Jerónimo decided that a priestly career was not for him. Instead he became a rural schoolteacher. Jerónimo became proficient in Latin and could speak French quite fluently. He possessed an artistic temperament and had quite a facility for drawing. He had a knack for composing verses and would sing them as he accompanied himself on the guitar or violin. He found an outlet for his music and versifying as a *pallador* or minstrel, and entered festivals in competition with other troubadours. He was fond of telling tall tales.

The young man began teaching in northern Chile. This land of contrasts had both its fertile and desolate areas. Stretching from the mountains and valleys of the cordilleras of the Andes to the Pacific Ocean, it was rich in folklore and served as a cradle for many notable poets.

PETRONILA

Jerónimo was teaching in the little town of La Unión when he became acquainted with a widow who had a fourteen-year-old daughter. Petronila Alcayaga de Molina was a small, delicate woman of great beauty. She had a soft, almost pathetic voice that had a marvelous quality of reaching the heart.

The teacher-minstrel fell in love with Petronila and pursued a brief and persuasive courtship. In 1888 they were married in the parish church at Paihuano.

When Petronila became pregnant, it was feared that she might have complications giving birth. As a consequence, they moved from the little village of La Unión to Vicuña, capital of the Valley of Elqui.

A DAUGHTER IS BORN

It was at four in the morning on the day of her parents' arrival in Vicuña that the future poetess-teacher was born in the small house at 759 Maipu Street. The infant was baptized the same day in the Church of the Immaculate Conception in Vicuña. She was given the name of Lucila.

Gabriela Mistral, whose true name was Lucila Godoy Alcayaga, was born in the province of Coquimbo, Chile, on the seventh day of April, 1889.

The first three years of Lucila's life were quite happy ones. Both parents adored her. Jerónimo, who doted on her, prepared a little garden for her, starting her on a quest for the beautiful that would last the rest of her life. He also wrote little cradle songs for her.

From hearing these songs in her infancy, Lucila, as Gabriela Mistral, would later write tender cradle songs for other children. She would remember the women folk of the little towns where she spent her childhood and recall the scene of a loving mother singing an infant son to sleep.

Lucila was a beautiful child with blue eyes that sparkled

The Early Years

when she smiled. But she was shy and reserved because she played alone so much. For companions she often resorted to domestic animals, insects, birds, and plants. Many times she would rush from her mother's arms to the little garden. There Petronila would find her daughter in intimate conversation with an iguana or with the birds and flowers. At other times Lucila would be in silent contemplation, observing the almond trees in bloom or other marvels of nature in the garden or in the sky above. Often she would make small figures of clay.

Petronila instilled in her daughter a love of nature. She also provided a warm and sheltered home life. Lucila would inherit many of the good qualities of her mother's Basque heritage, particularly her honor and tenacity. Lucila considered her mother blessed or holy, perhaps because Petronila had suffered so greatly to bring Lucila into the world. Later, as Gabriela, she would extend this religious sentiment to all mothers.

MARITAL DISCORD

While both parents adored their daughter, problems developed in their relationship with each other. Petronila would often interrupt her husband's vocal expression of his dreams and aspirations, with bickering, grumbling, recriminations, complaints, and impatience at his efforts to create instant rhymes.

Jerónimo was filled with an insatiable wanderlust and with the call to adventure. He would stay faithfully at home for brief periods of time. Then, when the urge was upon him, he would follow his natural bent for travel and adventure. He would leave the house for days at a time without explanation. Perhaps it was to escape an oppressive home atmosphere. He would seek elsewhere to gratify physical pleasures and to try to refine his mediocre talent as a poet. Later he would return home without any explanation, as if he had just stepped out to feed the chickens.

It was common in the village for an absent father to have become involved with another woman. Lucila's paternal grandmother left her husband because the grandfather had been caught sleeping with the maid.

Finally, in 1892, when Lucila was three, Jerónimo left home for the last time. The marital unhappiness of her parents left its mark on the mind of the child. Lucila knew that her mother suffered both from her father's presence and his absence. But Petronila refused to divorce him and continued to hope for his return and a change from his vagabond ways. She was also afraid of the effect that a growing resentment might have on the mind and spirit of her child. While her father's desertion of his family did cause serious changes in the life of Lucila, she did not blame her own suffering on him, though the girl would grow up in the midst of widows and frustrated wives who believed that men were inconstant and often unfaithful.

From her father Lucila inherited a love for the fantastic, a fondness for travel, and a passion for folklore. Jerónimo's parting legacy to his daughter included a handful of romantic poems, his background as a teacher in an elementary school, his love of nature and music, and his vagabond spirit of moving from place to place.

Since she now lacked the presence of an earthly father, Lucila would look for solace and guidance from a steadfast *Dios Padre* (Heavenly Father). He would be both stern and loving, righteous and merciful.

EMELINA

Emelina Molina de Barraza, Petronila's first child, like her stepfather, was a country schoolteacher. She had started teaching in 1889 and would continue for thirty years.

In 1892, Emelina, who had been widowed, was named teacher in the country school of Monte Grande, a small town situated in the center of the Valley of Elqui in the high Andes. After Jerónimo's departure, Lucila and Petronila moved there to live with Emelina.

After the death of her own daughter, Graciela, Emelina took over much of the care of her little half-sister. In only one month she taught Lucila to begin to read. Then she started with lessons in writing and arithmetic.

MONTE GRANDE

The town of Monte Grande was situated in a narrow valley, set in the cordilleras and surrounded by mountains. It was inhabited by a strong and tenacious people who had converted the valley into a beautiful garden. Here Lucila lived a life closely attuned to nature. Her eyes drank in the natural beauty of the landscape and of the stars in the heavens. Her ears took in the sounds of the wind whistling through the trees. She could hear the rushing of the waters being drawn by the villagers as they worked the soil.

Monte Grande became the home of Lucila's heart. It was the scene of her childhood. Here she learned to play, to reflect, and to be intimate with God and His creation.

The patriarchal customs of Monte Grande made life easier for the two women and the little girl. They represented nearly three generations, but they were united by love and hard work. They lived humbly, but not in disgrace, for in Monte Grande there was no separation of classes. The villagers lived as one large happy family. Petronila encouraged those with more than ample goods to best distribute the surplus among the needy. She often sent little Lucila to some neighbor to ask him for some apples, peaches, or other fruits to give to those who did not have any.

Lucila was fascinated by nature. In her pursuit of a mastery of it, she found an inexhaustible source of knowledge in Adolfo Irribarren, a well-to-do proprietor of Monte Grande.

Irribarren, like Lucila's mother, was of Basque origin. He had a deep interest in plants and animals. He had transformed his country estate into a true botanical and zoological garden. He allowed Lucila to play among his exotic plants and with the deer, gazelles, peacocks, and pheasants. He showed the young girl a world unknown to her; it was also largely foreign to the Valley of Elqui. He told Lucila stories of the different species and explained the various parts of the world. He also introduced her to the study of astronomy. All this helped to stimulate her young imagination.

CHILDHOOD DREAMS

Lucila did not completely lack companions of her own age. In later years, four girls who attended a one-room schoolhouse in Monte Grande would be remembered in a poem she wrote as Gabriela Mistral. With the braids of seven-year-olds flying and their bright percale aprons, they chased flights of thrushes among the shadows of pine and grape. Here in the Valley of Elqui, encircled by a hundred or more mountains, they dreamed of the sea. One day all would be queens and rule kingdoms by the sea. They would wed husbands who would be kings and poets like King David of Judea. Their dream kingdoms would include vast and fertile lands.

Gabriela recalled that none was ever to be a queen. The other three would always live away from the sea. Rosalie would kiss a sailor who was already wedded to the sea. But the one who kissed her would be devoured in a storm. Soledad would spend her life bringing up seven brothers and never even look at the sea. In the vineyards of Monte Grande, she would rock the sons of other queens, but never one of her own. Efigenie would meet a stranger on the road. She would follow him without a word or without knowing his name, for the man seemed like the sea.[1]

Lucila talked with the river and mountains and fields of cane; in the realm of nature she had a kingdom of her own. She counted ten sons in the clouds as she reigned over the salt marsh. She saw her husbands in the rivers and her royal train in the storm.

Thus the Valley of Elqui, among a hundred mountains or more, played host to the young maidens as they played and sang of their childhood dreams.

The Valley of Elqui and Monte Grande became for Lucila an earthly paradise which, as Gabriela Mistral, she would carry

The Early Years

forever in her heart. Images with which she became familiar there constituted the essence of much of her poetry. She loved the common people as a friend and preserved them faithfully in her memory.

VICUÑA

Lucila's tranquil and happy life came to an end when she was sent to spend the last year of primary school at Vicuña. Until that time she had been very comfortable studying in Monte Grande under the love and direction of her sister-teacher. Thus she had not recognized her timidity nor her need to overcome it.

The school at Vicuña was in the charge of Adelaida Olivares, a friend of Lucila's mother. Adelaida, who was blind, took the girl as her companion. Lucila accompanied her from home to school and back. She was assigned the task of distributing papers to the other schoolchildren, who wanted to receive their papers rapidly and derided Lucila for her slowness. Perhaps because Adelaida was blind, she did not realize how timid and sensitive Lucila was, how circumscribed and interior her previous life had been. These things conspired to place a heavy responsibility upon the little girl from Monte Grande.

Because she was new and shy, and because of her closeness to the teacher, Lucila was taunted unmercifully by her classmates. Even her name, Lucila Godoy, sounded something like "Totilla Llolloy." This and her slow actions caused the other children to make fun of her.

A crisis came when some of the teacher's papers were missing. Adelaida accused Lucila of taking them. The little girl from Monte Grande denied it, but Adelaida was enraged. She ordered Lucila out of the classroom and encouraged the other pupils to throw stones at her.

This first encounter with human cruelty left a deep impression on the future teacher-poetess. It helped her to understand that she would have to fight for the rights of the defenseless, the humble, and the poor.

Lucila was sent back to Monte Grande where she again found

in her sister Emelina the self-denial, devotion, and guidance that she so much needed at this time.

LA SERENA

Lucila spent the first twelve years of her life in the country, but in 1901 the family moved to La Serena, capital of the province of Coquimbo. La Serena, an old city rich in tradition, was on the Pacific coast at the entrance to the Valley of Elqui. It was here that Lucila had her first encounter with the sea. Its impact upon her was astonishing. The sea became for Lucila not simply an impersonal element, but a most powerful being with whom she conversed and which she called *Padre*.

She studied the formation of its waves, the color of the water, the rhythm of the ebb and flow of the tide and breakers. She then became involved in the separate elements that made it in total more than the sum of all its parts: the salt, the seaweed, the mariners, the little ships, and the fishermen. She sought to understand the sea, the gentle motion that could rock one to sleep, and its music that could give counsel, imbue happiness, and whisper the secrets of the universe. The sea became an important element in Gabriela's work.

GRANDMOTHER AND THE BIBLE

Also in La Serena, Lucila's paternal grandmother, Isabel de Villanueva, played an important role in the spiritual development of the young girl. She kindled her granddaughter's heart with an ardent and passionate love for God and eternal life. Isabel, a deeply religious woman whose family had come from Argentina, was the possessor of the only Bible in La Serena. She seemed to have the energy of the Basques, coupled with the fortitude and melancholy of the Indians and the tenacity of the Jews.

On Sundays, Lucila would be dressed up in her best clothes and taken to the home of her nearly blind grandmother. Seated by her side, Lucila would read to her from the Bible. Thus the girl became quite familiar with the book of Job, the Psalms, Ecclesiastes, the Lamentations of Jeremiah, the Song of Songs, and the Book of Revelation. This experience left a deep impression on Lucila's spirit and had a great influence on her future writings as Gabriela Mistral.

Because Job, David, Solomon, and the prophets were revealed to her as friends, it helped her to understand their struggles and suffering as they expressed their deep and violent passions for God. King David was her first great love. She spoke of him as *Father* and *Beloved* at various times.

In the New Testament, Lucila found not only food for her spirit, but also passages of passion and intimate tenderness, passages that were meaningful to her and her people. Scenes from the infancy of Jesus had a strong impact on her. Thus she learned to appreciate the simple things of life, to bear sadness with stoicism, to be both compassionate and gentle. Yet she also knew how to be angry at times.

A LOVE OF LEARNING

Despite economic difficulties, Lucila would, from that time forward, devour all the books she could find. An amiable Spanish shopkeeper loaned her some, and she was permitted to use the library of a well-to-do, generous neighbor. She also absorbed knowledge from the people and things around her.

Through constant study and effort, Lucila was becoming self-educated, though it was without any particular approach or design. She read whatever books fell into her hands, with no opportunity to select those that would guide her studies. She read some of the books of a then popular Colombian writer, José María Vargas Villa, who for a time and in some ways might be considered her teacher through his work. But his style was morbid and artificial and was ultimately neutralized by the sincerity and vital realism of the Sacred Scriptures with their vehement metaphors, scorching indictments by the prophets, and cries of deeply felt passions.

2
Emerging Poetess and Teacher

EARLY WRITINGS AND FIRST JOBS

Lucila wrote her first poem at eleven years of age; it was called "Lola" and dedicated to her friend, Dolores Molina.

Nevertheless it was probably at fourteen, in 1904, that she became determined to write more seriously. Then some of her work was published in *El Coquimba* (The Burrowing Owl) at La Serena and in *La Voz de Elqui* (The Voice of Elqui) at Vicuña.

Her first published writings contained a certain romanticism and socialism that the provincial society thought of as revolutionary. The result was that she was prevented from entering the Normal School at La Serena. At first she was admitted, but later turned away at the insistence of the chaplain, Ignacio Munizaga. This came as quite a bitter blow, for it meant that she could not pursue her studies there toward her dream of becoming a teacher. Long ago she had decided that teaching was to be the only career for her. She had inherited an aptitude for teaching from her father. Both her mother and her sister had encouraged her. After the first shock of not being admitted to the Normal School, the obstacle only served to strengthen her resolve. Tutoring by Petronila and Emelina helped her to outline a course of study and finish it outside of school.

The only avenue to teaching open to her at this point was to try to gain admission into the profession by way of practical experience. She secured her first job, that of clerk in the high

Emerging Poetess and Teacher

school, in La Serena in 1905. She was to assist the principal with the boys of the higher classes. But her deeply Christian concept of justice caused her to rebel against the lack of concern for the poor. She accepted as students some girls from homes in the lower classes; then she defended their rights. As a result she lost her job. In her desperation she turned again to the sea for counsel.

Lucila's distress came to the attention of the governor of the province. When he learned the cause of her anxiety, he saw to it that she was given a job as assistant in the rural school at La Campañia Baja, a community about three kilometers from La Serena. This was her first teaching post.

Here Lucila taught poor children by day and workers by night. She composed little poems to help the children learn to read. She was scarcely more than a child herself, but she understood the importance and beauty of her mission as a teacher. On Sundays the people showed their appreciation as they sang songs together.

This personal contact with the youth and the humble people of the working class unified Lucila's feeling of love for all of God's creatures, and she continued as a primary teacher from 1905 to 1910. Though in later years she would gain fame as a poet and diplomat, she always considered herself first as a simple rural schoolteacher who had written many poems and songs for her children, using the Valley of Elqui as a source. She taught for more than twenty years. By the end of those days she had become a spiritual guide to all who knew her.

LA CANTARA

In 1907, Lucila was transferred to the school at La Cantara. This was a little village of some thirty white houses, located between the port of Coquimbo and La Serena.

She was now a young woman of seventeen, tall with light hair, greenish blue eyes, and hands as delicate as a lily.

Lucila, using the pseudonym of "Alma," wrote for *Penumbras* of La Serena; David Bari, editor and publisher of the periodical, adopted a position of *avant-garde* in art. The young teacher also wrote for *La Voz de Elqui* and *La Reforma.*

From the beginning of her literary career in 1904, Lucila had been subject to critical attacks, with many diatribes hurled at her. Yet she faced them with fortitude and determination from an inward shell, or armor, of a high and indomitable character. She felt that to control these miseries with indifference and constructive energy would prove valuable in combating greater problems to come.

Although Lucila was writing some poetry, she was noted still more for her delightful and thoughtful prose. Carlos Soto Ayala, editor of *Literatura Coquimba,* described Lucila as "the intelligent prose writer whose pen of gold is dipped in ambrosia."[1]

During this period, Lucila read with fervor the works of the modernist poet from Nicaragua, Rubén Darío.

ROMANCE AND TRAGEDY

It was in La Cantara that Lucila experienced her first love affair. It was there that she became better acquainted with a young man she had met in La Serena the year before. Romelio Ureto was employed by the local railroad as a baggage clerk and conductor. Sometimes Lucila and Romelio would eat together in the local boardinghouse, where the young girl usually saved him a seat. Their close relationship was somewhat marred by frequent and bitter disputes over some sharp differences of opinion. Finally they broke off their relationship and parted.

Romelio imprudently had used some money belonging to the railroad to help a friend, Carlos Omar Barrios, but Carlos refused to repay the loan. Romelio was now in trouble. Unable to replace the funds, in a moment of desperation to uphold his honor, on November 25, 1909, Romelio placed a gun against his own temple, pulled the trigger, and died a suicide. On his body was found a postcard on which was written the name of Lucila Godoy.

Romelio died in Coquimbo, while Lucila was on a trip to Santiago.

SECONDARY SCHOOL TEACHER

The year 1910 marked a new phase in the teaching career of Lucila Godoy. She was teaching in Barrancas when, encouraged by her friend Fidelia Valdes and the poet Victor Domingo Silva, she went to the city of Santiago. Here at Normal School Number One she was allowed to take the examinations for a teacher's certificate which would let her teach in secondary schools. She was permitted to use the knowledge she had acquired in practical teaching without further formal study. The director of the school, Brigída Walker, perceived the sensibility and sensitivity of the young teacher and allowed her to write her first proof of botany in verse.

Lucila was ever grateful to this educator who helped her so much. Below are the opening lines of "La Encina," which later appeared in *Desolación,* her first volume of poetry and prose. This was a beautiful poem dedicated to the memory of Señorita Brigída Walker.

> The soul of woman strong
>   yet delicate,
> Compassionate in gravity,
>   serious in love,
> is a magnificent evergreen oak
>   of sweet smelling scent,
> for over its rough branches
>   creep a myrtle in bloom.

The Reverend Father Medardo Alduan, who knew Lucila at the time, wrote of her:

> I knew her in the year 1910, at twenty years of age, surrounded by little children, protecting them, with the fervor of motherhood, under the wings of her teaching profession.
> She looked at the children and observed humanity. For that, she ought to be presented to the literary world, without presumption, the name of Teacher . . . as an apostle of education, who is the most excellent character that we ought to recognize in the American poet.[2]

Lucila developed from a romantic adolescent to a young woman consecrated to her profession, completely devoted to her vocation as a teacher. She was interested in the encouragement of young minds and hearts and anxious to impart her knowledge and experience to others. She would help them in their studies and guide them on the road to truth, beauty, and hope.

The Chilean critic, Armando Donoso, wrote of her:

> She wished to establish hope and beauty into the hearts of children with such a love as a mother would have in speaking to her child.[3]

In 1911, Lucila taught hygiene for two months in the *liceo* (high school) of Traiguén. She was then named inspector general and teacher of history in the high school for girls at Antofagasta.

This appointment was probably made due to the influence of Tereso Prats Bello, inspector of primary education, who was interested in her and described her as a "young woman of majestic carriage, with beautiful green eyes, sparkling clear, with the hands of a princess."[4]

Pablo Neruda, who knew her when he was only a boy, remembered how the teacher-poetess had inspired him and relieved his anxiety to read by loaning him some books from her own library.

Although most of her time was devoted to teaching school, she spent many hours dedicated to study and meditation.

Among the friends she had in Antofagasta were Dr. Pedro Oligario Sánchez, rector of the Liceo Fiscal de Hombres, and Carlos Parrau Escobar, president of Destellos (Sparkles) Lodge, which was affiliated with the Theosophical Society, founded in India by Colonel Olcott and Madame Blavatsky. Due to the influence of the Orient, Lucila never included meat in her diet.

Lucila had attended mass and gone to confession as a young girl. Although she was essentially a Catholic, she was also something of a mystic in search of eternal truth and was attracted for some time by books on occultism or spiritualism. She occasionally attended meetings of the lodge at the home of Dr. Sánchez.

LOS ANDES

It was in May of 1912 that Lucila was named inspector general and professor of history, geography, and Spanish in the High School for Girls in Los Andes. It was in the pleasant atmosphere of this city, amid the peaks of the Cordillera, that she remained until 1918. During this time she wrote profusely. Generally she used the pseudonym of Gabriela Mistral. She worked under the direction of her friend Fidelia Valdes Pereyra, director of the school, a woman with a quality of deep understanding.

Lucila dedicated her poem "El encuentra hermosa" to her friend. It was published in the *Revista de Educación* in December, 1914.

In 1918 Lucila wrote of Fidelia's influence on her life:

> I have taught six years under the direction of Fidelia Valdes, the educator whose high and pure life has placed on me brief touches of light that I could not see in myself. . . . my sensibility, my limited ability, my great enthusiasm, all that I have given to the profession. I am poor. I have only the treasure of youth and I have surrendered it without reserve.[5]

In December of 1913 and March of 1914, Lucila contributed to *Nueva Luz,* a review dedicated to the Chilean theosophical movement. For it she wrote a poem, "El himno al arbol" (Hymn to the Tree), and a poetical essay, "La Charca." Both pieces had symbolic religious significance. The young teacher, who had a deep interest in all religions, at this time felt particularly close to some of the Oriental principles. For a time she believed in reincarnation. Below are a few lines of "Hymn to the Tree":

> Brother tree, that fastened
>   by brown hooks in the soil,
> your clean forehead is lifted up
>   with intense thirst to the sky.

The poem is like a prayer, revealing the tree's presence to the traveler who is refreshed by its shade and fragrant atmosphere.

The poetess asks that her own presence in life be revealed by her warm, gentle influence shed over others as silently as does that of a tree. She wants her heart and thought to be as fruitful as a tree. When deep unrest and fever of the century consumes her powers, she wishes to be refreshed and to be serene with the calmness of a tree.

She sees the tree as a woman's womb, for within its boughs and branches are nests, with a tiny life rocking gently in each cradle on its branches. The poetess asks for foliage deep and thick so that she may meet the needs of those in the human forest who have no branches to be their home. Just as the strong tree gives forth its sheltering and protecting grace, the poetess asks that her own soul in youth or age, joy or grief, give forth love unchanging, love for all.

Although the metaphor of a foliage-thick tree suited her, Lucila was not preoccupied with feminine adornment. It was characteristic of Lucila all her life to walk proudly erect with a rhythmic step as she dressed with the austere simplicity of a prophet. Later, in an article about the Statue of Liberty, she said that she preferred the loose and flowing robes of the ancients to modern dress.

The house in which Lucila lived in Los Andes had a small patio with an orange tree, a tomcat, an owl, and a dove who would serve as her companions during her meditations.

It was in Los Andes that Lucila became acquainted with Juana Aguirre de Aguirre and her husband, Pedro Aguirre Cerde, then minister of Justice and Education and much later president of the Republic of Chile (1938-1941). To these two friends her book *Desolación* would later be dedicated.

During the years spent in Los Andes, Lucila was emerging as a personality in the world of Chilean literature. In July, August, September, and October of 1912, she wrote for the review *Sucesos,* published in Valparaíso.

3
Growing Recognition

AN APPEAL TO RUBÉN DARÍO

In 1912, the same year her work appeared in *Sucesos,* Lucila sent a letter to Rubén Darío. She wrote with humility about her own ability and how much his own writings had meant to her. The letter, signed Lucila Godoy, was written in the diffuse orthography that Andres Bello, the educator, had popularized in Chile.

She asked that Rubén publish two of her works if he considered them worthy. The first was a poem, "El angel guardian." The second was a fable, "La defensa de la belleza," which later would be included in *Desolación* under the title of "Porque las rosas tiene espinas."

Both pieces were published in March and April of 1913 in the literary review *Elegancias,* under the pseudonym of Gabriela Mistral. This was the first time any of her work had been published outside of Chile.

The opening lines of "The Guardian Angel" introduce the idea of a Guardian Angel:

> It is true, it is not a
>   story;
> there is a Guardian Angel
>   who takes you and carries
> you like the wind,
>   and goes with children
> wherever they go.

The Guardian Angel has soft hair that blows in the wind. His solemn, sweet eyes quiet you with a penetrating look; they blot out your fears with their brightness. He has a body, hands, and winged feet. Though you may be asleep, his six wings carry you through the air. He makes the ripe fruit sweeter; he cracks the nut from its shell.

He sets you free from gnomes and witches. He helps you cut roses ensnared in a bed of thorns. He carries you over rough waters and sets you on the highest crag. Though he is at your side, when sin puts its mark on you, he leaves your body and gathers up your soul.

There is a Guardian Angel. It is not a story, the poetess assures us. He goes with children wherever they go.

In her fable "Why Roses Have Thorns," Lucila delights her readers with a tale.

In times long past, roses, like many other plants, were common because of their excessive number and the places in which they were located. No one would believe that roses, today's princesses, had been made to beautify the roadside. Yet it is so, nevertheless.

God walked through the land one hot day. When He returned to Heaven, He was heard to say:

> The roads of this poor land are desolate. They are ugly with their dry clods and bareness. The sun punishes them and travelers who trod them. I have seen men driven mad by the heat.

The roads were important as a connecting link between remote villages, so God continued:

> It would be good if we could make fresh camps for those who travel these paths, and give them beautiful visions, shelter, and reason for happiness.

God then made the willows, which bless with their inclusive arms, which project protective shadows for some distance. He made roses in full dress, covering the bare walls along the roadside.

Merchants and other travelers looked at the willows as they passed beneath them. Sometimes they stopped in their cooling shade and shook the dust out of their sandals.

They smiled as they discovered the green covering with its blanket of white and yellow roses on the roadside walls. As they sniffed the sweet fragrance of the flowers, their beasts neighed happily. There came up from the roads, piercing the silence of the countryside, songs of strange mysticism.

But men, as has happened before, abused the things entrusted to their care. Although the height of the white poplars were their defense, and the faded branches of the willows held no particular attraction for those who passed below, the roses, on the other hand, smelling with an Oriental fragrance, were as vulnerable and appealing as a little girl in the mountains.

In a month of life, the roadside was barbarously mutilated and among the flowers there were many wounded roses. But flowers were women who did not suffer their martyrdom in silence. Their complaints were carried to the Lord. Trembling with anger and very red, a poppy spoke:

> "The men are ungrateful, Lord. They do not merit your grace. From your hands, in a little time, they have destroyed integrity and beauty. We wish to be rasping to man, for he has carried out wastefully as we opened up our petals to give more perfume. We tire from drawing up the strength from our roots to be fresh."

A shepherd passed and said that they appeared red, and bowing down, doubling, as the queens of the story. He rooted out a jasmine with a great stalk.

An old pilgrim passed. He shaded his ancient brow and failing eyes, exclaiming,

> "Praise be to God for such snowy creatures, Lord, for you are glorified."

Then came our most beautiful rose. A little rascal passed, saying:

> "What convenience! Flowers by the side of the road."

He grasped a branch of roses and withdrew, singing, as he walked up the pathway. The roses pleaded:

> "Lord, such a life is impossible. In a few days the roadside will be as bare as before. We will have been destroyed."
> "What do you wish?"
> "Defense. The men protect their gardens with teeth of thorn or bramble. Something of the same you could do for us."

The good God smiled with sadness, because He had hoped to create benevolent beauty. Then he said:

> "Let it be. I see that I may have to do the same. Men have power to inflict hostility and hurt."

Now the roses are smooth and harmless in outer appearance, yet from them rises up sharply, in defense, the thorn. And man, always unjust, said afterward that God had altered the goodness of his creation.

LOS JUEGOS FLORES (THE FLORAL GAMES)

In 1914 the Society of Artists and Writers of Chile, a literary and political organization, sponsored a poetry contest and invited all young writers in Chile to respond. There were four hundred entries. Lucila Godoy was encouraged by her friends to take part. Her entry consisted of three poems called "Los Sonetos de la muerte" (The Sonnets of Death). They were entered under the pseudonym of Gabriela Mistral.

The jury of poets included Manel Magallenes Mourse, who presided, Armando Donoso, and Miguel Ángel Rocuant. "Los Sonetos de la muerte" were received with enthusiasm. They were of a tone new and distinct and, in turn, passionate, violent, and intimate. They won first place in Los Juegos Flores, the national contest.

It was on December 22, 1914, that the award—Laurel Crown and Gold Medal—was to be given to Gabriela Mistral. The scene was the Santiago Theatre. But Lucila Godoy was too shy to accept the honor in person. A fellow-teacher from the same school in Los Andes came to receive the award on her behalf. He expressed regret that the poetess could not be present.

While Victor Domingo Silva, a Chilean poet, read aloud the three poems of "Los Sonetos de la muerte" to the audience, Lucila Godoy Alcayaga, too shy to make her presence known, sat in the balcony listening to the reading of her poems, watching the proceedings on the floor below.

There are reasons to believe that the three sonnets that make up "Los Sonetos de la muerte" were written in 1909, a year after the death of Romelio Ureto. There is evidence that the poetess did not wish for them to be published at that time.

These sonnets, which crowned her literary triumph, show a familiarity and almost an obsession with death that might be attributed to the tragedy.

Although most of the standard biographies of Gabriela give 1915 as the date of her father's death, one account shows that Jerónimo Godoy Villanueva died of pneumonia in the Coiapó Hospital on August 29, 1911.

Thus we see that Gabriela's childhood experience and familiarity with suffering and death, as well as her adolescent conflicts and the deaths of Romelio and, possibly, Jerónimo had an impact on much of her poetry.

THE PSEUDONYM

It was after the recognition of the Floral Games in 1914 that the pseudonym, Gabriela Mistral, was permanently adopted and used the rest of her life. Previous pseudonyms had been Alma, Alquien, X, and Soledad. In the years to come, *Gabriela* was the name by which the poetess would be belovedly known to a vast Latin-American audience.

There is some disagreement as to the source and meaning of Gabriela Mistral. Virgilio Figuera, who wrote her first biography, said that Gabriela represented the *spirit* and Mistral the *breeze* of the earth. Some feel that it is a combination of the given name of Gabriele D'Annunzio and the surname of Frédéric Mistral. Both of these European poets were among Gabriela's favorites. Others believe the combination comes from the archangel Gabriel and the mistral, the wild wind that sweeps across the Mediterranean, thus uniting heaven and earth in the name. In general, Gabriela would represent the presence of the archangel Gabriel; Mistral would represent her love of nature, as shown in the recognition of the strong and powerful Mediterranean wind, as well as her admiration for Frédéric Mistral, her beloved French poet.

INCREASED RECOGNITION WITHIN AND OUTSIDE CHILE

After her literary triumph in the Floral Games, many visitors came to Los Andes to see Gabriela Mistral. Many prominent figures in the world of literature carried on a correspondence with her. The principal writers of Latin America—Amado Nervo, Enrique González Martinez, José Vasconcelos, and many others—expressed an interest in her work.

Understanding the struggles and suffering of the young woman, Amado Nervo used the term *sister* in speaking of her. He considered her to be one of the finest poets of modern times.

In the letters she wrote during this period of her life, Gabriela revealed a spontaneity and a constant desire to be of help. She considered herself a teacher. With all due modesty, she felt a deep responsibility to take part in the intellectual development of the young generation. She felt her mission was to guide each of its members toward a more spiritual and idealistic world.

In a letter to Eugenio Labarca, Gabriela wrote:

> I have one aspiration: I believe I have received a mission in this little bit of earth: to move away from materialistic philosophy that lately has an intense involvement in Arts and Education.[1]

She continued to feel an empathy toward all men with religious sentiments and to write about the humble and distressed of the world and to dedicate to them beautiful articles and poems. She wrote:

> Many times I think of writing something in praise of the high spirits and unknown who are the salt of the earth, and the light of the world, as the parable says.[2]

She lamented the destruction of spiritual values in the literary world of Chile. She discussed with her friends writers in whose works moral principles were similar to theirs. She admired literary works that contained profound ideas because, for her, ultimate gratification was found in truth, understanding, and the best in fine arts.

She wrote on one occasion, "I love beauty and I kneel before her wherever she is."[3]

Writers mentioned in these discussions with friends included Delmira Agustini, Maria Monvel, Alone, Andreiff, Azorin, Darío, Dostoyevski, Emerson, Gorky, Guerra, Maeterlinck, Nervo, Romain Rolland, Shakespeare, Rabindranath Tagore, Tolstoy, Turgenev, Unamuno, and Winter.

Gabriela seldom wrote about her own work. Nevertheless she told Eugenio Labarca that she would like to write a book of verses for children to be entitled "Versos escolares."

An article by Labarca about Gabriela was published in *Primrose* (Chillán) on February 21, 1915. He wrote about her wishes:

> She desired to create a new type of poetry for children that ought to be artistic and impregnated with the lively breath of God.[4]

Gabriela had told Labarca:

> I wish to create a new poetry for pupils that is not what it ought to be for children, that it ought to be more sensitive whatever else, deeper, of things of the heart, more stirring in inspiring the soul.[5]

She thought of publishing a second book to be called "Los Sonetos de la muerte." As it turned out, this would be her first book and would appear under the title *Desolación*.

In some of the letters that Gabriela wrote are indications of her sincerity and independence of character:

> As a teacher of children, I am sincere. I know that to speak the truth in treating a subject is to make it worthwhile, for I am a teacher of children. One speaks the truth and it remains worthwhile and satisfying. If there is anything of value in me, it is not my bad verse or bad prose; it is my sincerity, nearly forgotten, my loyalty to mine, my impossibility to hurt anyone.[6]

In a letter to Nataniel Yanez Silva, she defended a literary group called "Los Diez." But she maintained her independence of all groups with these words: "I am a person outside."[7]

She fled from praise. At the same time, she said in beautiful phrases, she would prefer a simple and sincere expression of friendship.

> I like little or no praise in public, but what pleases me more than the daily articulation of exaggerated praise is a loyal letter from a man or woman of delicious spirit.[8]

Although she was only twenty-six years of age, she wrote to Rubén Darío that she felt she was an old woman whose purpose in life was to guide and educate young people.

After her triumph in the Floral Games, the name of Gabriela Mistral crossed the frontiers of Chile. Her works in verse and prose appeared in many literary reviews, at times without any authorization or acknowledgment. It is important to note that she would constantly correct her work until she arrived at a text that was acceptable to herself, and she was unhappy to discover in print her poems in a form she did not like. During all her life she felt the need to correct her writings. Toward that end she effected changes, minor and fundamental, in books twenty years after their publication.

While her name appeared in Chilean literary reviews that included *Pacifico Magazine, Figulinas, Sucesos, Primrose, Luz y Sombra, Familia, Ideales, La Sombra, Los Diez,* and periodicals on the American continent reproduced her songs, Gabriela continued to live modestly in the little town of Los Andes.

Gabriela made a short visit to Santiago where she was interviewed by Isaura Dinator de Gúzman, who described her.

> She appeared to me as a young woman radiant of youth who possessed beautiful green eyes. She had a fair complexion and pleasing features.[9]

Much has been said of Gabriela's personal appearance, the aristocratic dexterity of her hands, the beauty of her eyes, and the soothing effect of her warm and generous smile.

The husband of Isaura, Manuel Gúzman Maturana, educator and writer, lived in an educational and literary center. He perceived Gabriela's grandness and asked her to write some poems and prose to be used in a five-volume series of textbooks. Thus some fifty-five of her works in poetry and prose were included in *Libros de Lecturas de Gúzman Maturana* between 1916 and 1918. These books were used in many South American countries and helped increase Gabriela's fame inside Chile and outside in the neighboring countries.

Three of Gabriela's commentaries in prose and some of her verses were included in *Rabindranath Tagore, poeta y filosofo hindu* of Raul Ramiriz, a book published in Santiago in 1917.

Nine of Gabriela's poems appeared in the anthology *Selva Lirica,* compiled by Juan Agustin Araya and Julio Molina Nunez, that was published in Santiago the same year.

As her popularity increased and with it some turmoil, Gabriela found moments of peace in her work with young people. She wrote:

I wish to recover my strength for my work, my only reason for living. To the children, I have given myself and only for them I guard my health and my efforts. I am a spinster devoted to the sons of others.[10]

DISAPPOINTMENT IN LOVE

Not long after her first literary triumph, according to Margot Arce de Vasquez in *Gabriela Mistral: The Poet and Her Work* (New York: New York University Press, 1964), Gabriela met, under romantic and somewhat strange circumstances, a young poet from Santiago. She felt for him a passion that was deeper and more intense than her first love for Romelio. Some time later he married a young lady from Santiago's high social circles. This was a bitter blow for Gabriela. Her frustrations and sufferings are reflected in some of her poems.

In a personal letter dated October 20, 1961, to Martin C. Taylor, author of *Gabriela Mistral's Religious Sensibility* (Berkeley: University of California Press, 1968), Margot Arce de Vasquez, confirmed the existence of this second love affair, which was not disclosed in the earlier biographies. Out of respect for the wishes of the poetess, she did not reveal the name of the person, who was still alive.

Professor Margaret Rudd, the author of a biography of Miguel de Unamuno, one of Gabriela's favorite Spanish philosophers and writers, is in the process of writing a biography of Gabriela. She has completed the first volume, which covers up to the year 1922. She suggests that the other person was probably Jorge Hubner, the Chilean poet.

Thus, there is evidence pointing to two different persons and episodes as subjects for the poems of tragedy, disappointment, frustration, and bitterness that later appear in *Desolación*.

Certainly Romelio's suicide weighed heavily upon her. In "El Ruego" (The Prayer) she carries her plea that Romelio be forgiven directly to God. Although she was well aware of the teaching of the Roman Catholic Church regarding the death of a person who died a suicide, she did not believe that the final desperate act of Romelio would not be forgiven.

Growing Recognition

You know, Lord, with what fiery boldness,
Your help for strangers I have asked.
I come now to plead for one who was mine,
My cup of freshness, the honeycomb of my mouth.
....
Do not turn your back when I plead with you,
    for one who was mine.
....
He was a good man; I tell you
    that he had a heart
        open as a flower in bloom.
....
You tell me sternly, that he is unworthy of my pleas,
since he did not anoint with prayer his fevered lips,
and he went away that evening without waiting for Your
sign, his temples shattered like a fragile vase.
....
You say that he was cruel?
You forget, Lord, that I loved him,
and that he knew my heart was wholly his.
That he has troubled forever
    the waters of my happiness?
It does not matter! You know:
    I loved him, I loved him.
....
Here I rest, Lord,
my head bowed down to the dust,
talking with you through the twilight,
or through all the twilights
    that may reach through life,
if you are long in telling me
    the word I hope for.
....
I shall wear out your ears
    with prayers and cries,
like a timid dog licking
    the hem of your garment,
and your loving eyes cannot avoid me,
nor your foot escape the hot rain of my tears.
Speak at last the word of forgiveness.
....
The eyes of the wild beasts will be wet with tears,
and the mountain you forged from stone
will weep through its white eyelids of snow;
The whole earth will know you have forgiven.

Although it may not be totally valid to read into Gabriela's poetry the reflection of her life, "La Espera Inutil" (The Useless Wait) may give us a glimpse of her emotional feeling in the period of adjustment after Romelio's death.

> I had forgotten that your light foot
>   had turned to ashes,
> and as in good times past,
> I started out to meet you on the path.
> ....
> The sun had broken into bits
>   like a scorched dead poppy;
> flocks of mist trembled over
>   the dead countryside.
>   I was alone.
> The autumn wind creaked
>   through a whitened tree bough,
> I was afraid and called out to you,
>   "Beloved, hurry your step!"
> ....
> I forgot they had made you
>   deaf to my pleading,
> I forgot your silence,
>   your whiteness in death.
>
> I forgot your still hand
>   not reaching for my hand,
> I forgot your eyes staring wide
>   with question supreme.
> ....
> I shall not call out to you again
>   for you no longer walk here,
> My naked foot must travel on,
>   but yours is forever still.
> It was in vain that I kept this
>   appointment on these desert paths.
> I cannot bring to life again your
>   person in my own empty arms.

Gabriela felt jealousy and bitterness at the collapse of her second love affair. Though the wind was sweet and the path full of peace, her eyes were wretched as she saw him pass by with another. In "Dios Lo Quiere" (God Wills It), Gabriela expresses her bitterness:

> The earth will be a hateful stepmother
> if your soul should sell my soul,
> The world was more beautiful when you made me
> yours as we stood wordless beside the thorn tree.
> There love like a thorn pierced us like a thorn
> with its fragrance,
> Now the kiss you give to another echoes in
> my ears and returns to me in your every word,
> As the dust of the road holds the scent of
> your feet, like a deer I shall track you over
> the mountains,
> Though you creep to the corners of the earth
> to kiss her, you will see my tear-stained face!

Disappointment in love was especially bitter for Gabriela, because it meant that she would remain childless.

Gabriela always wanted a son of her own, but it was not to be. Her "Poem of the Son" reveals the intensity of her desire.

> A son, a son, a son!
> I wanted a son, yours and
> mine in those days of ardent
> ecstasy when my bones would
> tremble at the least sound of
> your voice, and my brow would
> beam with a radiant mist.

Yet fear that the son of one who had proved unfaithful might also turn against her is also revealed in her poem. She will never have a son of her own.

Gabriela resolves to turn to the teaching of sons of other mothers and, trusting in God to fill her grainary with grain divine, she closes with a prayer:

> Our Father, Who art in heaven,
> lift up this supplicant and let
> me be Yours, if I should die
> tonight.

4

Flight to Forget

PATAGONIA

When the object of Gabriela's affections married another, it was a cruel blow that caused her to ask for a transfer to a new location, hoping in this way to overcome her frustration and disillusionment.

In 1918, she went to Punta Arenas, on the Straits of Magellan, to become director of a school for girls. In this inhospitable region she remained for two years in voluntary exile. She was fleeing from the places where she had lived the terrible drama of her disappointment in love.

Desolate, her wounds still fresh from cruel memories, she expressed this suffering by writing poetry that described the bleakness of the new landscape. Here was an endless white plain near the Antarctic region with howling winds and foggy skies. The long night was filled with phantoms.

This southernmost tip of Chile had nothing in common with the fertile beauty of her native Elqui Valley with its fruitful abundance of orchards, the clearness of its rivers, and the warm brisk breezes that drifted through the trees.

Yet it was in Punta Arenas, today's Magallanes, that Gabriela's great love for Patagonia was born. She called it the land that the world had forgotten. In speaking of it later, she would say that at least she had seen the midnight sun. She would record with affection the frigid and stormy region with its dense forests and cordial people.

Flight to Forget

> I have traveled through the most desolate region of my country through Patagonia near the Antarctic. The climate is hard and it is very cold, but the people are warm and good. Yet, I remember with care, that here was the beginning of the terrible rheumatism that I have had through the years.[1]

The sculptor Laura Rodig, who had known Gabriela in Los Andes and accompanied her to Patagonia, was impressed with the cooperation and dedication the young poetess gave to social works in the region.

Gabriela knew the humble and the defenseless, and she never abandoned them. She visited the prisons and the hospitals. She helped materially and spiritually small children, especially those who suffered from malnutrition or rickets.

One time she said, "I want to give myself fully to popular education."[2]

Trees were planted for her in the Avenida Colón and in the Plaza de las Punta Arenas, and they remain there still, tall and strong, as a mark of her short but unforgettable residence in the place.

All the places that Gabriela visited exerted an influence on her and left their mark on her personality and her work.

Laura Rodig remembered how Gabriela would write her impressions, as sketches in small books. Some of the titles were "Los pajaros de Chile," "Las mariposas," "El folklore," "Yerbas "medicinales"—proof of her intense interest in nature. Other titles included "Los hebreros," "Voces indigenas," "Inglés," and "Francés."

A good part of what appeared in *Desolación* was written in Punta Arenas. What inspired the title of the book is a small island of the same name, which was very near.

Pacifico Magazine of Santiago published "El niño solo" in September, 1919. Her article "El pueblo hebreo" appeared in *Renacimiento,* a Jewish review of Santiago in November, 1919.

"El pensador de Rodin" and "El niño solo" were published by Cervantes of Madrid in January, 1920. This firm had begun publishing some of Gabriela's work in 1917.

TEMUCO

In 1920, Gabriela Mistral was named director and professor of Spanish in the Liceo de Temuco, which she had organized.

It was here that she was inspired to write poems of the sad, unfortunate people, when, in a poor section, she saw a pregnant woman trembling from the vile comments of a passerby. Gabriela felt a closeness to all of her sex and believed that she had a mission to reveal the true religious significance and holiness of motherhood. She declared:

> It is one of us who must show, what men have not said, the holiness of this beautiful and sorrowful state. It is the mission of art to show all the beautiful, in a great mercifulness, that which has been purified, to the eyes of the impure. These are dedicated to the women capable of seeing that the holiness of life begins in motherhood and for that reason is sacred.[3]

Laura Rodig recalls the trip with Gabriela on the Rio Imperial where they stayed a day in Puerto Saavedra at Lake Budy as guests of the poet Augusto Winter. Then, in Temuco, they came in close communication with Pablo Neruda, the poet who later was to be awarded the Nobel Prize. Laura writes of the latter association:

> Both formed a friendship, a symbolic alliance, geography and spirit of Chile, going both ways before the world, as a great song of two voices.[4]

SANTIAGO AND LICEO NUMBER SIX

That same year, 1920, Gabriela was transferred to Santiago to become the first director in charge of Liceo Number Six, founded in May of that year. It was the highest post in secondary education. For this school, Gabriela wrote eighteen maxims that reveal the purity of the rules of conduct that in her opinion ought to guide teachers, as well as stating her religious conception, nearly a mission, of teaching. Several are listed on the opposite page.

Flight to Forget 33

> All for the school, very little for ourselves.
> To teach always—in the patio and in the street, as well as in the classroom.
> Do your job well each day. It is not enough to do good just on special occasions.
> In order to correct, do not be afraid. The poor teacher is the teacher with fear.
> All can be said, but it should be said with form. The most severe reprimand can be made without humiliating or poisoning the spirit or soul.
> The teaching of children is the highest form of finding God, but it is also the most terrible in the sense of tremendous responsibility.
> Idle chatter is dangerous from the teacher with the pupil. It is beautiful when there at his side, the teacher always has something of value to point out to the class.
> Each lesson is sensitive of the beautiful.
> Nothing is sadder than that the pupil might confirm that his class was equal only to the textbook.[5]

Gabriela placed all her confidence and hopes in children, because she thought through them the world would be made purer. She wrote: The children bring me confidence in a world purer and more just than it actually is.[6]

Meanwhile, in June, 1921, Gabriela's "Poems of the Mothers," explaining the religious significance of maternity, was published in the *Repertorio Americano* of San Jose, Costa Rica.

On one occasion, she said of these poems, which were written in poetic prose,

> They were almost unedited, for I gave them to a review that only circulated among teachers, the *Review of National Education*. They were published with success in Buenos Aires. I was afraid, and I fear, they will scare pious women, because they are clear; they are crude.[7]

When the director of the school sanctioned a law that prohibited the naming of a teacher without a university degree, Gabriela resigned her position.

5

A New Career, Another Country

INVITATION TO MEXICO

It was at this time that Don José Vasconcelos, Secretary of Public Education in Mexico, passed through Chile. He had been representing Mexico in activities organized for celebrating the day of independence for Brazil. He became acquainted with Gabriela and in an interview asked her to come to Mexico to aid in the reformation of the educational system there.

In June, 1922, Gabriela left Chile for the first time and began a new career, accepting the invitation by the Mexican government to collaborate in the educational reform in a moment when the country was experiencing a spiritual and artistic renaissance. When she arrived in Mexico José Vasconcelos was in the process of organizing the department of the Secretary of Education with few tools but much spirit. The revolution had triumphed over the dictatorship and Obregón was now president.

Vasconcelos wished to keep the spirit of liberty alive, with all young people, particularly, being given the fruit of it. All this was necessary after twelve years of war, especially since the civil war was not quite over as there were still some armed factions here and there in the north.

In the capital, Vasconcelos had arranged the publication of the Greek classics, Plotinus, the Gospels, and the *Divine Comedy*. The Amphitheatre, decorated by Diego Rivera, was crowded with people listening to the symphonies of Beethoven. Now was the

A New Career, Another Country

time to restore justice and culture. At last it was propitious to meet the needs of the people hungry for bread and culture.

As soon as Vasconcelos learned that Gabriela had accepted the invitation to come to Mexico, he summoned Palma Guillén to his office, where he told her:

> "Palma, Gabriela Mistral is coming here. She is going to work with us and I want her to know Mexico well. I want her to see the good and the bad, that which we have and that which we lack. Do you know who Gabriela is?"[1]

Palma admitted that she knew very little about the Chilean poetess-teacher. She had read the "Sonnets of Death" in a literary review, but had heard nothing of the teaching and social work or of the other ideals of Gabriela, nor of what they signified on the American continent. The Secretary of Education went on:

> "She has some very good ideas on education. She is a woman of the countryside and the country. She knows the needs of the people in the rural areas. She is a great teacher and a great poetess. I have thought much about whom I should have accompany her and guide her. I do not want her to get a confused or partial picture of Mexico, nor do I want her to see only the good or only that which is of interest to the person who guides her. I want Gabriela to see all that she may, give us her opinion of what we are doing, and help us through her experience and intuition. I think that you can be most useful for this mission. You will journey with her, make her to know the country, the beautiful and the ugly, the capital and the province, all the countryside, the university and the rural school, and all the rest."[2]

PALMA GUILLÉN

Palma was then a teacher in the normal and preparatory schools and had been working with Vasconcelos in the organization of popular libraries in the capital, the primary schools, and the centers of education, and in choosing who ought to travel to the rural missions throughout the country. Palma wrote:

> I confess the mission was not very easy. Gabriela was a person quite different from myself. She knew much of many things, and had learned all on her own without teacher or school. She was a teacher, and so was I. She taught the Spanish language and geography. I taught literature, psychology, and logic. What a *diverse* climate was ours! She had lived in America, but had read, translated into Spanish, many classic and modern writers. For her, it was America, Latin America, that was important. I was nearer to Europe, to France, than to Colombia or Argentina. I knew more of Homer, Lucretius, Schopenhauer, or Bergson than of Miranda, Sarmiento, or Rodó. However, my courses in Spanish-American literature with the great teacher Pedro Henriquez Urena helped to supply me with the memory of many verses of Darío and José Asunción Silva. Nevertheless, she was a grand poetess, and grand poetesses at times move in an atmosphere beyond the simple mortals of character; above all, she was a woman of the mountain; I was a woman of the plain. In Gabriela, there were many obscure zones, deep and mysterious, "that she would know of ashes and sky!"[3]

Little by little, Palma began to understand Gabriela as she learned more things about her. Respect increased to affection, because Gabriela seemed so alone and abandoned.

Gabriela arrived in Mexico on a ship that had taken her from her native soil for the first time. She was received at the port in the name of the secretary by Jaime Torres Bodet and Palma Guillén. Palma wrote of her first impression:

> I do not know what impression Gabriela made on Jaime Torres Bodet. To me she was a presumptuous girl; she appeared to be badly dressed, bad belt with large, ill-fitting skirts, her low shoes and her hair gathered in a low knot. I saw Gabriela's timid eyes. Those eyes, covered with almost closed eyelids, had two ways of looking. A look, rapid and lightning-like in which there could be enchantment, surprise, anger or fear, very frequently of fear; and a serene look. They seemed sustained like enchanted water, as a green water filled with too much light. They had the look of confidence, of comprehension, or repose, but most of the time her eyes were like those of a frightened bird.[4]

Palma admitted:

> I did not know in those nearly two years in Mexico that I was near the happy Gabriela: her country manner of laughing, her delight to make jokes, witticisms, imitations, and caricatures, nor her gift, quite common so much later, to make me laugh so much. The Gabriela who arrived in Mexico, in 1922, was the one who wrote in Punta Arenas in a night of untied wind, "El Poema del Hijo."[5]

GABRIELA IN MEXICO

More than forty years later, after the death of Gabriela, Palma wrote of their experiences in Mexico together from 1922 to 1924.

They went together side by side, from one end of Mexico to the other: Pachuca, El Chico, Cautla, Cuernavaca, Puebla, Taxco, Zacapoaxtla, Attixco, Patzcuaro, Zamora, the Cañon of Tomellin, Oaxaca, Acapulco, Guadalajara, and Veracruz. They traveled through sun, dust and heat; to schools installed in old parishes, in patios, manor houses, and houses without furnishings. They traveled in trains or trucks of the Secretary of Education, sometimes sleeping in them. When there were hotels or boardinghouses, they stayed in them. At times they found lodging in the best house in the city or village. They met with chiefs, school inspectors, rural teachers, and professors.

In Pachuca, they were guests of Señora Bustamente and her daughters, Anita and Dora, friends of Gabriela until her death. There Gabriela became acquainted with Lolita Arriaga, the rural teacher of Zacapoaxtla, of the famous Recado.

At times they were accompanied by Gabriela's secretary, Eloísa Jaso, sister of the great teacher, Carlota Jaso. Sometimes it was just Palma and Gabriela traveling alone.

Some believed that Gabriela received much money in Mexico and spoke of her exorbitant salary; some said she came for pleasure and received her salary without work—none of which was true. Gabriela, in her own country, was director of a high school, that is to say a preparatory school. In Mexico, she had the title of inspector, with a salary nearly equivalent to but somewhat less than what she had in Chile. Her traveling expenses from one part to another were paid, but nothing more.

The Secretary hired two high school teachers who had come with Gabriela—one as a teacher, the other as a professor of drawing.

Gabriela lived in a little house that she rented in Mixcoac and modestly furnished it from her own salary. At times when she stayed late in the city because of unending conversations, she would sleep at the home of Palma's mother or the home of Señora Jaso.

Gabriela went often to the villages, and the country people loved her. She spoke with the teachers and saw them at work. She held conferences with them on the true meaning of education, about books that would be of help to them, books for children and young people, the use of libraries, the culture necessary for the teacher and the woman; she spoke of her native country so distant, yet so close to Mexico.

Gabriela loved Mexico with a love born of knowledge and hope. She was a better propagandist for and defender of Mexico than it had ever had before. Later, the name of Mexico was always on her lips. Her memory of Mexico, after her stay there, was constantly revealed in her poems.

People in villages and cities came from all over to be near her and to listen to what she had to say, with true religiosity. She was very intuitive and immediately established contact with her audiences. She knew just how to establish the tone that would make her theme interesting and understandable. She visited stores, workshops, and offices. She spoke with teachers, with the workers, and above all, the women.

DESOLACIÓN

It was while Gabriela was in Mexico that her first volume of poetry was published, but it was not published in Mexico or in Chile,

A New Career, Another Country

but in New York, where Dr. Federico de Onís, professor of Spanish literature at Columbia University, had stimulated interest in Gabriela's work. According to the professor, his students wanted to know where they could get her poems, but all he could give them was a handful of clippings. He told them that if they wanted her works collected in a volume, enough of them would have to subscribe to pay for the printing.

Dr. Onís made contact with Gabriela in San Angel, Mexico, and at his insistent persuasion, she prepared a collection of her work in prose and poetry and sent it to him in New York.

Thus, the Spanish Institute of the United States, founded at Columbia University in New York in 1920, published her first book, *Desolación,* in 1922. The first edition carried this dedication: "Edition dedicated by the author to the teachers of Spanish in testimony of admiration and affection."

She further dedicated the book to her friends Pedro Aguirre Cerda and his spouse, Juana Aguirre de Aguirre, to whom she said, "I owe the hour of peace in which I live."

Contained in the volume were poetry selections, including "Life," "The School," "Childhood," "Sorrow," "Nature," and "Cradle Songs." Included in the section on "Sorrow" were the "Sonnets of Death" and the "Poem of the Son." Included in the prose passages were the "Teacher's Prayer" and the "Decalogue of the Artist."

At the close of the book, Gabriela asked forgiveness of God for such a bitter book. She vowed that in the future she would try to write words of hope and mercy that would bring consolation to men. She wrote, "At thirty years, when I wrote the 'Decalogue of the Artist,' I made this wish. May God grant me the life to complete it."

Gabriela's conception of beauty is revealed throughout the "Decalogue of the Artist."

1. You shall love beauty, for it is the shadow of God over the universe.
2. There is no atheistic art. Although you may not love the

Creator, you acknowledge Him by creating His likeness in your work.
3. You shall not create beauty just to excite the senses, but to give nourishment to the soul.
4. You shall not use beauty as an excuse for luxury or vanity, but as a spiritual exercise.
5. You shall not search for beauty or offer your work at carnival or fair, because it is virginal and not to be found there.
6. Beauty shall rise up from your heart in your song, and the first to be purified will be you.
7. The beauty of your work shall call forth compassion and bring comfort to the hearts of men.
8. You shall bring forth your work as a mother delivers her son, from the blood of your heart.
9. Beauty shall not be an opiate that lulls you to sleep, but an excellent wine that fires you to action, for if you do not respond as a man or woman, you will not be an artist.
10. All your creation shall leave you with humility, because it is less than your dream and inferior to the dream of God, which is in nature.

Gabriela's creed was expressed in a poem that she wrote while she was quite young. "I believe in my heart," she wrote. "Why? Because it has been created by God, who dwells in it forever."[6]

Besides this, she believed strongly in and lived her life by the precepts expressed in her "Teacher's Prayer":

> Lord, You who taught, forgive me that I also teach and bear the name of teacher, the name you bore on earth.
> Give me such a devoted love for my school that not even a glowing vision of beauty can rob me for a moment of its tenderness.
> Master, make my devotion long lasting and my discouragement brief. Root out from me this improper desire for justice that still disturbs me, this petty spirit of protest that rises within me when I am hurt. Let me not be saddened by the lack of understanding of others or pained by the forgetfulness of those I teach.

A New Career, Another Country

Let me be more mother than the mother herself in my love and defense of the child who is not flesh of my flesh. Help me to make one of my children my most perfect poem, and leave within him or her my most melodious melody for that day when my own lips no longer sing.

Show me that Your Gospel is possible in my time so that I may not falter in my daily or hourly struggle to make it live.

Let your shining radiance descend upon my school as it did upon the barefoot little ones who surrounded you so many years ago.

Make me strong in my weakness as a woman, a poor woman. Enable me to scorn all power that is not from You and all pressure which is not Your ardent will upon my life.

Friend, come with me! Sustain me! Many times I will have only You at my side. When my doctrine becomes purer and its truth deeply scorching, the worldly will abandon me, but You will press me against Your heart which knew the meaning of loneliness and being forsaken. I will seek only the sweetness of Your approval.

Grant me simplicity and intensity; free me from being too complicated or yet too simple in my teaching.

As I enter the school each morning, let me rise above the hurt in my heart. Let me not take to my work my earthly cares or the sorrows within.

Keep my hand light in punishment and tender my caress. Let me reprimand with sorrow, knowing I have corrected with love.

Help me to transform my humble school of bricks and stone into a spiritual temple. Let the flame of my enthusiasm find its way through the entrance and fill the whole room.

May the goodwill of my heart and endeavor provide a stronger support to it than the stoutest column and finest gold of the rich schools.

And, finally, let me be reminded from the painting of Velásquez, how teaching and loving held deep meaning for You, so that You arrived at that last day on the Earth with the spear of Longinus thrust into the heart while You still burned with love.

GABRIELA AND GUY INMAN

In 1922, with the stress and storm of economic disturbances and the rising of nationalism in all parts of the world, America was better able than ever to be of help to the world. Excluded from the council table a few years before, Latin America had recently taken its place there as well as in the economic world. Now she furnished the League of Nations with its president, with two of the six elected members of its council, and two of the eleven members of the World Court of Justice. A present question now was whether Latin America would cast her lot with Europe or whether all the Americas would work unitedly with other nations for the peace of the world.

An analysis by the Committee on Cooperation in Latin America (CCLA), of which Samuel Guy Inman was executive secretary, did indicate some encouraging signs of promise on the horizon in spite of a century of misunderstandings between the Americas.

While pointing out many indications of promise of closer friendship and understanding, Dr. Inman mentioned a sentiment that needed to be overcome. He told of the two things that, according to the Chilean poetess Gabriela Mistral, had united the South Americans: The first was the beautiful Spanish language; the second was the hurt caused by the United States.

LA NUEVA DEMOCRACIA

The commentary by Dr. Inman spoke of an organ representing Christian opinion before the Spanish-speaking world:

> The publishing of *La Nueva Democracia* is in some ways the greatest single achievement of the Committee. It has long been recognized that such an organ was necessary for reaching the educated classes of Latin America. No single society could command the finances, or sufficient representation of all the forces, to publish such an organ. The Evangelical work has been dignified throughout Latin America because of the review. Its articles are copied by the leading publications of America and Spain.[7]

La Nueva Democracia was begun in 1919 as a cooperative enterprise. Initial financing was furnished by the Interchurch World Movement. Editorial and business management was provided by the CCLA. Samuel Guy Inman was chosen as managing editor and director. Dr. Juan Orts Gonzalez, a member of the Literature Committee, was the first editor.

The first number of the publication appeared in January, 1920. On its cover was a map of both continents bound together in a circular frame on which were pictures of Washington, Bolívar, Columbus, and San Martín,

Gabriela soon began to be a regular contributor to *La Nueva Democracia*. In November, 1922, an editorial on Gabriela's work was printed in *La Nueva Democracia*. In December of the same year an article by her entitled "Various Classes of Books" appeared. In the January issue which followed, there was a study of Chilean poetry that had been written by Gabriela. The next month included her article on Mexico and the United States. Many of her articles and poems appeared in the publication for more than twenty years.

The Contents was divided into four sections:

1. *Sociologia y Moral* (Sociology and Ethics)
2. *Ciencia y Inventos* (Science and Inventions)
3. *Arte y Educación* (Art and Education)
4. *Cronica Mundial* (World Chronicle)

La Nueva Democracia, a Spanish publication, printed largely in the Spanish language, had within its four-page cover of the first issue thirty-two large, attractive pages filled with Spanish prose. The general format was carried through for the twenty-six years that *La Nueva Democracia* appeared as a monthly publication. Following a brief suspension, after the close of the Second World War, it resumed its mission as a quarterly similar in size and format to the *Reader's Digest*. It finally ceased publication in January, 1963, in the Memorial Edition honoring its last editor, Alberto Rembao, who died on November 10, 1962.

A CHAMPION OF WOMEN

The second edition of *Desolación* was published in Santiago in 1923 with a poetical prologue by Pedro Prado.

That same year, at the encouragement of José Vasconcelos, Gabriela completed an anthology of prose and poetry by various authors that included some of her own works, published or unedited. The book, titled *Lecturas para mujeres destinados a la ensenanaza del lengueje* (Reading for Women Emphasizing the Education in Language), was published in Mexico in 1923 under the auspices of the Secretary of Education. Twenty thousand copies were printed.

Then Vasconcelos decided to name a new school that had just opened for Gabriela Mistral: Escuela Hogar (Home School) Gabriela Mistral. The new school would emphasize the importance of the woman and the mother; and would be dedicated to honor the Chilean educator.

Orators honoring her on the occasion were the poets Jaime Torres Bodet and Rafael Heliodoro Valles. Copies of the new book were also distributed.

AROUSED CRITICS

Nevertheless, while Gabriela had traveled much in Mexico and was able to identify well with the people and their problems, there were some teachers, some very good teachers, and some writers in the capital who could not forget that they were nationalists, and very much *Nationalists*. They were disgusted, dismayed, and somewhat offended by the fact that a stranger—*Extranjera*—had been summoned to work in Mexico, and they made malevolent comments.

> Who would come to teach that we are not superior? What novelties has she introduced? Here are many good teachers and among them are those who could do in the country what Gabriela has done.[8]

A New Career, Another Country

The critics again pursued their prey:

> The name of a stranger, a living person, on a school in Mexico?[9]

The wave of criticism increased when it was learned that the sculptor Ignacio Asúnsolo was preparing a statue to place in the patio of the school named for Gabriela.

> A statue of a living person? What is so glorious about her? What has this woman done that is so extraordinary?[10]

It was in July, 1966, that Palma Guillén wrote from Milan in her introduction to *Lecturas para mujeres* (Editorial Porrua, S.A., Av. Republica, Argentina 15, Mexico, 1971) that

> I write this because Gabriela was not informed of these miseries. She knew the spiritual unity of Mexico. She knew how to love it as her own country; with what admiration and with what enthusiasm she lived among us, and the happiness she had each morning to see the sky of Mexico.[11]

But finally she learned of the criticism. Filled with sadness, she decided to leave Mexico. The invitation to work in Mexico would end in November, 1924, with the administration of Obregón, but she did not wish to remain until that time.

6
Life Abroad and Further Recognition

VISITS TO THE UNITED STATES AND EUROPE

Gabriela Mistral visited the United States for the first time in 1924. On the thirteenth day of May, she paid her respects to the Pan-American Union in Washington, D.C. Mrs. H. A. Coleman, president of the National League of Writers in the United States and one of the orators of the day, spoke of Gabriela. She declared that the teacher-poetess of Chile had been destined to be an apostle of truth who had dedicated her life to the welfare of humanity with her work to benefit children.

Gabriela for her part, spoke of her pride in her race, for the equality of the Indian, of the mission of the United States, and of religion. She said that among the men who had influenced her character was Emerson, who, for her, illuminated the blind passages of the human spirit.

The United States as a literary theme appeared for the first time in 1922. On the eighteenth of September of that year, she published an article, "Mexico and the United States," in the *Reportorio Americano* of Costa Rica. In this article, dedicated to the North American students who were attending the summer school of the National University of Mexico, she wrote of the necessary friendship between Mexico and the United States. She praised Mexico warmly and urged the students to know it and love it. She begged them to make Mexico known to their countrymen when they returned to their own land. She pointed out that

"Mexico is the arm that Spanish America extends towards the United States in a desire for justice and understanding."[1]

She asked the students for understanding and justice for South America. She asked them to lend their good will and efforts to the work of building continental peace. She told the students that she had found in the gesture of the North American teachers who had paid for the publication of her book an example of what love and unselfishness could achieve. She said:

> My book is at this very moment being printed in the presses of New York and it will be presented to me as a material and spiritual gift by teachers who understood the soul of their teacher without having seen her face.[2]

After Gabriela's speech on the brotherhood of the Americas which she delivered in Washington, she made her first trip to Europe.

In the latter part of 1924, Gabriela visited France, Italy, Switzerland, and Spain. Many beautiful articles recorded this period of her life: her interview with Giovanni Papini, her description of the Mediterranean, Naples, Florence, Majorca, and Castile.

TERNURA

Also in 1924, the Editorial Calleja, of Spain, published *Ternura* (Tenderness), her second book of poetry. The PEN Club of Madrid held a banquet in her honor in which she was seated as a guest between the president of the institution, Ramon Pérez de Ayala, and María de Maetzu. Also at the table were Concha Espina and the poet Enrique González Martinez, minister from Mexico to Spain. The Spanish critic Enrique Diez Canedo pointed out the austere graciousness and universal friendship that her work illustrated. The final tribute was paid by María de Maetzu.

Gabriela's second book of poems is a collection of children's poems. The book opens with a dedication to her mother and her sister, Emelina, both of whom had such a great influence on Gabriela's spiritual formation and her choice of teaching as a career. *Tenderness* contains seven sections: "Lullabies," (Canciones de cuna), "Rounds" (Rondas), "The Raving Woman" (La devariadora), "Tricks" (Jugarretas), "Story World" (Cuenta Mundo), "Almost for School" (Casi escolaries), and "Stories" (Cuentos).

The title, Tenderness, indicates the general character of the book and the principal emotion that is the source of its poetry. These poems sing of the pleasure of motherhood, the miracle of having a child, the charms of little animals, and the loving understanding between the earth and its creatures.

Themes of *Tenderness* include most of the elements of Gabriela's poetry—maternal love with its pleasures, enchantments, fears, and fantasies; the child with its games and legends; nature and the earth with its landscape, and the heavens and their constellations; matter including animals, vegetables, minerals, and things made by man; toil, America, sleep, death, peace, cosmic harmony, Jesus Christ, and God the Father.

Gabriela's children's poems have the same depth and intensity of emotion as her adult poetry. Their qualities reflect the mischief, malice, and playful grace of rhythm. She shows love and respect for the memory of children as she tries to discover the secrets of their souls, the intensity of their attention, and their imaginative and creative energy.

Gabriela knew of the problems of this sort of writing for children and tried to solve them. She was aware of her successes and failures. Among the difficulties was her struggle with language, while she tries to overcome what she called "verbal hybridization."

Speech, she wrote, is, after the soul, our most precious possession or perhaps we have no other possession in the world. Let the one who experiments with it and knows he is experimenting rework it as he pleases.

The Cuban Jorge Manach made this just and decisive evaluation:

> This art of speaking to childhood is one which only those who have a deep sense of the spiritual and concrete can

master. The fusion of tremulousness and plasticity, of the malice of beautiful expression with the innocence of emotion; what faultless achievement in the pages of *Ternura!*[3]

In *Selected Poems of Gabriela Mistral* (Baltimore: John Hopkins Press, 1961), Doris Dana speaks of Gabriela's deep sense of the eternal in *Tenderness*. She points out the poetess-teacher's lifelong dedication to her teaching vocation. Here are beautiful lullabies that Gabriela called "colloquies the mother holds with her own soul, with her child, and with the Earth Spirit around her, visible by day and audible by night."[4]

When *Ternura* was published, there was no body of children's literature in Latin America. According to Gabriela, it was still in its "swaddling clothes." Gabriela hoped to encourage such a development with this book. She created these poems partly to encourage others to write for children, partly to savor again the delights of her own childhood, and partly as a voice for other women. She tells us that the past is an undoer of knots and love without words is a knot that strangles.

Doris Dana has pointed out some of the extent of Gabriela's influence through her poetry:

> To this day in every classroom throughout Latin America, wherever little children learn to read or write, the voices haltingly pronounce the syllables of these verses. On every playground from Mexico to Patagonia, Latin American children of all races join hands in a circle and dance their *rondas* and sing the lyrics of the poems of *Tenderness*.[5]

Gabriela Mistral wrote, "Love that stammers, that stutters, is apt to be the love that loves best. That is what my love seems like, that I have given to children."[6]

MONTEVIDEO CONFERENCE

In the spring of 1925, an important gathering was held in Montevideo, Uruguay. In *Ventures in Inter-American Friendship*, Samuel Guy Inman, executive secretary of the CCLA and the managing editor and director of *La Nueva Democracia,* reviewed its purpose and proceedings:

> The eyes of the Christian world were upon Montevideo in those memorable ten days in March and April, 1925. Not only did those interested in the missionary progress of Christianity center their attention on Montevideo, but also those who were anxious about the international relations of the world.[7]

Organized under the auspices of the CCLA, the Congress on Christian Work in South America brought together representatives of eighteen nations, thirty-five organizations, and some seventeen denominations. Dr. Inman pointed out:

> This was a great spiritual adventure unparalleled in the history of the continent in which a large number of North Americans set forth to discover new friendships on the southern continent.[8]

A challenge for its deepest spiritual consideration was presented to the conference in a letter from Gabriela Mistral. It began:

> I am with you in these days of your Assembly, as well as your evening meetings, as you are thinking of two themes equally dear to you and to me, the School, and the Religious Character of our people. From the other side of the line, among the Catholics, there are a few voices which mingle with yours and one of them is mine.
>
> May God Himself preside over your Assembly and enrich you with great and clear thoughts. In these obscure and vacillating times, we have great need of the Divine Grace. As yet, we are afraid of many ideas which, like enthusiastic youth, seem to us too lively. It is necessary that we admit them to our counsels and permit them to present their case. Some of them are the social ideals which as yet find no place in our legislation—daring pedagogical ideas which bring with them a new set of values.[9]

In regard to the religious discussion of the relationship between Protestant and Catholic values, Gabriela wrote:

> I beg of you, with respect, but with vehemence, that you try to bring about an approximation with Catholicism, in order that we may undertake a common task. There are no less than ten ideas in which we are in complete agreement. We work, Protestant and Catholics, around the vertebral column of Christianity; let us seek more ardently our common points than our differences. In these days when some are talking about such debatable questions as the yellow peril, let us think of the great Christian opposition to materialism.[10]

Yet it was not the philosophical doctrine of materialism that disturbed Gabriela so much as materialism as a norm of conduct. Gabriela went on:

> The philosophical doctrine of materialism does not cause us so much uneasiness; that which troubles us and challenges us to unity is materialism as a norm of conduct, materialism loosening sanctions, lowering education to the level of economic training, sinking its teeth into international relationships, counseling the oppressions of the weak, and ever reaching out to our religions, to kill the mystic element in order to leave only tradition; materialism in the woman who flees from maternity as an economic burden and regards childhood as a high-priced merchandise; materialism in wealth, when it takes refuge in its pagan right to deny a living wage; and finally, materialism in the State when it hides behind the idea of liberty in order to maintain such institutions as legalized prostitution.[11]

The challenge to the spirit of the conference and its members is presented as Gabriela wrote:

> The Spirit exists though we trod it underfoot. Such ideas with which to defend the culture is born of the Spirit; study arguments with which to defend religions as the vital breath of nations; disentangle, so far as you may, the net of deception which is weaving itself about our youth, in order to relegate religion to the corner of worn-out rubbish. Such relationships between the Gospel and the present hour make clear the fact that it is full of power to purify human life. Defend also, my friends, the Spirit which exists in Art, and try to create a kind of international legion against the uncleanness which clings to the exhibition of beauty in the cinematograph, in the novel, in the painter's brush.[12]

"One of the painful phases of Latin American life," wrote Gabriela, "at the moment is the absolute divorce which is taking place between the popular masses and religion, or, perhaps better said, between democracy and Christianity."[13]

She cried out against the liberal leaders who had thrown aside all religion:

> They have not understood that religion is one of the aspects of culture which has contributed to the purification of the soul of the people. They have rejected religion as a factor of individual as well as social education, wrongly confusing religion with superstition.[14]

Gabriela touched on the attempt of the Russian people, with whom she found a parallel to the Latin American situation, to entirely do away with religion as she wrote:

> A faith which has nourished so many generations cannot be easily uprooted. The duty of the Christian is not wrathful denunciation, but to make a sharp analysis, as one who has suffered defeat, in order to see wherein lay the weakness of a sentiment which we believe to be eternal. I, who am firmly ingrained in Catholicism, after years of doubting, have set myself to do this with an aching heart for what my faith has lost, but at the same time with a clear mind, desiring rather to understand than to condemn.
>
> What I have seen is this. Our form of Christianity, contrary to that of the Anglo-Saxon form, has divorced itself from the social question, indeed has disdained it, and has held a paralyzed or dead sense of justice, until this sense has risen up in others and has taken the Church's following away.[15]

Gabriela contemplated on this tragic neglect and offered a challenge to help overcome it:

> A faith which began miraculously among the common people and which only very slowly won its way among the powerful ought never to have forgotten its source, but, which respecting this popular tradition, it ought to have seen that, entirely apart from religion, the so-called common

people, are for their very number the only soil which can maintain it. Other classes, however solid they may be, give it poor support. Wherefore, neither by tradition nor careful calculation has Christianity been loyal to her humble followers. We must not lose so many souls, however much our own souls are worth, God could not pardon the abandonment of multitudes who fill almost the whole world. Catholicism must regain what, either by neglect or selfishness, she has lost, and this will be possible if Catholics show that they are capable of renunciation, or are capable of the very essence of her teaching. The hunger for justice awakened in the people cannot be satisfied by a few meager concessions. The people know that they will gain the essential reforms without her help. Their attitude is not that of trembling supplication. We must accustom ourselves to the new accent among the popular masses. Whatever good can be done, it will cost Catholicism and Christianity, in general, the sacrifice of material interests. We will either make the sacrifice or we declare that we accept the teachings of Christ only as a beautiful bit of writing in the Gospel, or as a transcendent philosophy which raises human dignity, but that it is not for us a religion that is made of life. If we are to be dilettantes, esthetic reciters of parables for their pure beauty, it is well that we confess our Epicureanism. We shall remain, then, among the literary or philosophical commentators of religion. If we are to be that other, whole-hearted Christians, with a whole Gospel, we will go to the people.[16]

"Our religion," warned Gabriela, "must not restrict itself to mere worship, not even to the highest individual perfection. There must be in it that desire for totality which there is in all great movements of thought or emotion. The social sense in our epoch is vibrant in everything, from education to architecture. Shall Catholicism be exempt from such a desire without belittling herself?"[17]

FRANCE

In 1926, 1927, and part of 1928, Gabriela traveled through France, Italy, and Switzerland, accompanied by her friend, Palma Guillén. She worked and wrote wherever she went.

The Chilean government had named her as its representative

in the International Institute of Intellectual Cooperation. This was an organization that was a part of the League of Nations with its headquarters in the Royal Palace of Paris.

Gabriela was placed in charge of the section on Hispanic-American literature. She published a collection of Hispanic-American classics translated into French in several careful, critical editions, with prologues, annotations, and in some cases with glossaries. She was also a member of the Educational Cinematrophic Institute of Rome. During this period she lived at the Montpensier Hotel near the Royal Palace.

In February, 1927, she lived in a small house in the country, near Fontainbleau, in order to escape from the big cities. She stayed at the Montpensier Hotel for meetings of the Institute.

In May, 1927, Gabriela went to Provence, the land of Frédéric Mistral, from whom she had taken her name. For a while, she lived in Bédarrides, a little town there. It was here that she prepared her work on Latin America for the institute.

During 1927, Gabriela represented the Association of Teachers of Chile in a Congress of Educators at Lucarno. She also assisted in the Congress for the Protection of Children, which was held in Geneva, Switzerland, the same year.

The letters she wrote to Benjamin Carrion while abroad reveal her constant love for Spanish America, her admiration for its writers, and her desire to be useful. Her passion for books and the desire to guide her friends caused her to recommend the works of writers that she considered to be important.

With Victor Andres Belaunde, then technical advisor of the institute, she founded the collection *Spanish-American Classics*.

The collection was created to familiarize the French-speaking public with the principal Latin-American writers through translating their representative work to reflect the best that was in America, its culture, and its folklore.

At the beginning, it was proposed to publish the works in French, Italian, English, and German, but lack of funds caused the program to be curtailed and the collection was published only in French.

SPAIN

In the autumn of 1928, Gabriela went to Spain to assist the Council of University Women as a delegate from Chile and Ecuador. She stayed in the Residence of Young Ladies, of which her friend Maria de Maetzu was in charge. There for the first time she met Margot Arce de Vasquez, who would later write a book on Gabriela. The original Spanish edition appeared under the title of *Gabriela Mistral: Persona y Poesia* and was published by Ediciones Asomante in San Juan, Puerto Rico. It has been translated into English by Helen Masslo Anderson under the title of *Gabriela Mistral: The Poet and Her Work* (New York: New York University Press, 1964).

Miss Arce remembers her first brief encounter with the poetess in the golden garden of the young women's International House.

Some of the delegates had been talking under the trees when Gabriela came toward them with her remote air and the tiredness of centuries. A woolen cape that fell below her knees emphasized her movement, like that of the eddying of a river. The radiance of her sharply etched head helped to compensate for the stolidity of her body. Her eyes and mouth seemed to contradict each other. It was a mouth bitter with worldly knowledge, yet the eyes were serene and inquisitive.

In her poem "The Stranger" (La Extranjera), Gabriela reveals a magnificent and moral self-portrait. She insists in speaking of her "apartness," the constant sensation she felt of strangeness and isolation with which she had lived for several years in a small Provencal village:

> She speaks in her way of her savage seas
> With unknown algae and unknown sands;
> She prays to a formless, weightless God,
> Aged, as if dying.
> In our garden now so strange,
> She has planted cactus and alien grass,
> The desert zephyr fills her with its breath,
> And she has loved with a fierce, white passion

She never speaks of, for if she were to tell
It would be like the face of unknown stars.
Among us she may live for eighty years,
Yet always as if newly come,
Speaking a tongue that pants and whines
Only by tiny creatures understood.
And she will die here in our midst
One night of suffering,
With only her fate as a pillow,
And death, silent and strange.

LEAGUE OF NATIONS

On September 26, 1928, the counsel of the League of Nations appointed Gabriela to an important post in the administrative department of the Instituto de Cinematografia Educativa in Rome, created thanks to a generous subsidy granted by the Italian government.

During her stay in Italy, Gabriela prepared the material necessary for an Italian version of *Sleeping Beauty* of Charles Perrault.

In 1928, Gabriela returned to Provence, to the small city of Bédarrides in Vancluse between Orange and Avignon. The country house she lived in, called Villa Saint Louis, had a large garden filled with fragrant greenery. At the entrance to the garden a sign read "Property of the League of Nations." Gabriela spent part of her time watering the plants in the mornings and cultivating them with tender care. Gabriela would travel as necessary to help in meetings in Paris, Geneva, and Rome.

Among the young writers who benefited from her spiritual direction were Andres Iduarte and Jorge Carerra Andrade.

Iduarte, who lived in the house from the eighteenth of April to the eighth of August in 1929, compared Gabriela to Saint Teresa for her unending fight for justice. At times her conversation would be earthy, and at times heavenly. Her preoccupation with and her love for humanity made it impossible for her to isolate herself from life around her. She saw in social Christianity the salvation of mankind.

Life Abroad and Further Recognition

Iduarte and Carerra Andrade, who lived close to Gabriela at this time, remembered that she went to church every Sunday. She believed in the power of the devil, and, owing to her mysticism, she left aside all worldly preoccupations. She imposed strict discipline on all who surrounded her, giving her and her home a religious tone and an austere atmosphere. Yet she could laugh, and when she did her smile illuminated her face and softened her features.

Gabriela had the gift of purification; all who were near her were attracted by her spiritual world, desiring it or not. Andrade spoke of her:

> In a lowly flower bed of her garden, Gabriela Mistral with her ample figure, her hair gathered in a knot, her walk slow and solemn, found herself in an appropriate atmosphere. A holy gardener who moved in a clear war against disorder, barrenness, and death, in defense of truth, love, and life.[18]

Gabriela considered herself permanently in this world as an exile, a condition which was self-imposed. She sought spiritual perfection and disdained the luxurious. She did not wish to belong to a single country, but to all. She imposed upon herself a constant moving about in the world.

Nevertheless, she did not wish to pass through any country as a simple visitor. She felt the necessity to absorb all that each country could offer, refine it and arrange it to make it a part of herself. Gabriela needed always to continue her march in search of perfection, carrying with her the memories of all the nations she had known.

JUAN MIGUEL

In Bédarrides, Gabriela had with her a nephew, Juan Miguel, aged four, whom she tenderly called "Yin-Yin," and on whom she lavished a maternal love. There also was Pradara Urquista, a young Chilean woman, who looked after the house.

Martin C. Taylor, author of *Gabriela Mistral's Religious*

Sensibility (Berkeley: University of California Press, 1968), tells how Juan Miguel came into Gabriela's life.

In 1929, while serving as consul in Madrid, Gabriela learned that a Carlos Miguel Godoy, accompanied by a baby, was applying for a visa to Chile. The relationship of the baby to her father, Don Jerónimo Godoy Villanueva, was soon made clear. Carlos was the son of Jerónimo by an extramarital liason. Martha Mendoza, mother of Juan Miguel, had died of tuberculosis in Barcelona. Carlos, revealed as Gabriela's half-brother, voluntarily surrendered the child to Gabriela for permanent care. Upon this orphaned nephew, Gabriel showered great affection. He helped to fill her maternal need and to satisfy her longing for a child. Thus, she obtained, though vicariously, the motherhood previously denied by her promise to remain true to an unattainable lover and her distrust of physical love.

ALICE STONE BLACKWELL

It was in 1929 that *Some Spanish American Poets* was published in New York and London. Included in the volume were prose and poetry selections by Gabriela Mistral. The texts were both in Spanish and translated into English by Alice Stone Blackwell.

Alice was the daughter of Lucy Stone and Henry Blackwell. Lucy Stone was a pioneer in the fight for women's rights. Henry Blackwell was active in the fight against slavery. Both worked together in the movement for Women's Suffrage up until the time of Lucy's death.

With this background, Alice continued in the struggle for Women's Suffrage on up through the early part of this century. She also spoke out against the oppression of people elsewhere, which included the Jewish pogroms in Russia.

Alice's first and only love affair was with an Armenian student, that ended when the young man died prematurely. Together they translated Armenian poetry into English. After his

Life Abroad and Further Recognition

death Alice continued to translate into English poems concerning the unfortunate minorities in Eastern Europe. She joined *Friends of Armenia* and spoke out against the perpetrators of the Armenian massacres.

In the introduction to her translations of Spanish-American poetry into English, she relates an incident that took place during the Mexican Revolution. It showed the high regard that Latin Americans held for their poets.

During a skirmish the soldiers of the defeated party broke and fled. One of the fugitives climbed a tree, but the pursuers came up and leveled their guns at him. He called out, "Do not shoot me! I am a poet!" At once the guns were lowered, and he was allowed to go.

Among the prose pieces in the volume, under "Poems for the Home," were Gabriela's reflections on "The Lamp."

> Blessed be my lamp! It does not overwhelm me, like the blaze of the sun, and it has a softened glance, of pure gentleness.
>
> It burns in the middle of my room; it is its soul. Its subdued reflection hardly makes my tears glitter, and I do not see them as they run over my breast.
>
> According to the dream that is in my heart, I change its little crystal head. For my prayer, I give it a blue light, and my room becomes like the depths of the valley, now that I no longer raise my prayer from the bottom of the valleys. For my sadness it has a violet crystal, and makes things suffer with me. It knows more of my life than the breasts on which I have reposed. It is alive, because it has touched my heart so many nights. It has the soft warmth of my inner wound, which now does not burn, which, because it has lasted so long, has become very soft.
>
> Perhaps, at nightfall, the dead, who have no power of sight, come to seek it in the eyes of the lamps. Who can that dead man be, who is gazing at me with so much silent gentleness?
>
> If it were human, it would grow weary in the presence of my suffering, or else, full of solitude, it would wish to be with me still when the mercy of sleep comes. Then it is perfection.

> It is not to be perceived from without, and my enemies who pass believe that I am alone. To all my possessions, as small as it, as divine as it, I give an imperceptible brightness to defend them from the thieves of happiness.
>
> Enough for me is what its halo of brightness illumines. It has room for my mother's face and the open book. Let them leave me only what this lamp bathes in its light; they may dispossess me of all besides!
>
> I ask of God tonight that no sad soul lamp dim the brightness of its tears!

In another of the "Poems of the Home," Gabriela writes of "The Earthen Jar."

> Earthen jar, dark as my cheek, how easy of access you are to my thirst!
>
> Better than you is the lip of the spring, open in the ravine; but it is far away, and on this summer night, I cannot go to it.
>
> I fill you, slowly, every morning. At first the water sings as it falls; when it remains silent, I kiss it on its tremulous mouth, paying for its gift.
>
> You are graceful and strong, dark jar. You are like the bosom of a countrywoman who nursed me when my mother's breast failed. I remember her when I look at you, and I feel your outline with its tenderness.
>
> Do you see my dry lips? They are lips that hold many thirsts for God, for beauty, for love. None of these has been like you, simple and obedient; and the three continue to make my lips white.
>
> As I love you, I never set a cup beside you; I drink from your lip itself, holding you in the curve of my arm. If in your silence, you are dreaming of an embrace, I give the illusion that you have it.
>
> Do you feel my tenderness?
>
> In summer I put you under fine sand, golden and damp, to keep the heat away from you, and once I covered a little break in you softly with fresh clay.
>
> I have been slow in my many labors, but I have always loved to be the sweet mistress, who takes hold of things with a trembling gentleness, if perchance they understand, if perchance they suffer, like her.

Tomorrow, when I go to the field, I shall gather sprays of mint to bring to you and submerge in your water. You shall smell the field in the odor of my hands.

Earthen jar, you are kinder to me than those who call themselves kind.

I wish all the poor may have, like me in this burning noon, a cool jar for their sorrowful lips!

Included in the poems on nature, translated by Alice Stone Blackwell, is "The Thorn-Tree," revealing a personal relation to her own suffering.

The thorn-tree fastens to a sterile rock,
Its form, contorted, barren, loved of none.
It is the spirit of the desert waste,
Twisted with pain and with the burning sun.

The oak is beautiful as Jupiter,
The blooming myrtle is Narcissus fair;
They made the thorn-tree like a Vulcan lame,
The frightful blacksmith God of hideous air.

They made the thorn without the lacy veil
That shrouds the quivering aspen, bright as leaf,
So that the spirit of the wayfarer
May not be conscious of its bitter grief.

Out of its matted tresses spring forth flowers;
Thus came to Job the gift of poesy!
Its scent is like the psalm the leper sang,
A fragrance piercing keen and pungently.

But though its odor fills the glowing air
Of noonday hours when all men take their rest,
In its dark hair it ne'er hath felt itself
Stirred to sweet trembling by a trembling nest.

The thorn has told me that it knows me well,
That on a night of anguish and of woe,
Against its myriads of wounding points
My heart was bruised and mangled long ago.

> Then I embraced it like a sister sad,
> As Hagar might clasp Job, oppressed with care,
> In an embrace that is not tenderness,
> But, alas! It rather is despair.

In "Prayer for the Nest," the poetess reveals her love for nature and consideration for the helplessness that needs protection.

> Sweet Lord, I for a brother make my prayer,
> The nest, defenseless, innocent and fair!
>
> From its small feathers rise delicious trills;
> On its wee cushions birdlings learn to fly.
> And song, thou sayest, is a thing divine,
> The wing is of the heavens blue and high!
>
> Soft be thy breeze that rocks it to and fro,
> And soft thy moon that silvers it by night;
> Strong be thy branch upholding it in air,
> Beauteous thy dew that lends it jewels bright.
>
> Oh, from its dainty, delicate wee shell,
> Woven from ravelings red, with care and pain,
> Turn thou aside the frost's chill, glassy ice,
> The pebbles of the fiercely pelting rain.
>
> Oh, turn aside the wind's impetuous wing
> That might destroy it with a rough caress,
> And turn aside the glance that seeks for it,
> Eyes all on fire with evil eagerness!
>
> Thou who dost blame me when I martyrize
> Thy creatures delicate and dainty fair,
> The lilies with their fragile cups of snow,
> The tiny pinks whose purple warms the air.
>
> Oh, guard its form with gentle tenderness!
> Touch it with love, set on its branch apart!
> It trembles in the wind, as 'twere a child;
> The bird's nest bears the semblance of a heart.

Gabriela reveals her protective love for unfortunate children as she pleads for them in "Little Hands" and "Little Feet."

LITTLE HANDS

> O little hands of children,
>   That beg insistently!
> Of all the world's fair valleys,
>   The lords are ye.
>
> O little hands of children,
>   Extended towards the tree!
> For you the fruits that ripen
>   Glow ruddily.
>
> Yours the full combs of honey,
>   Breaking on every hand,
> And men pass by and see you,
>   Nor understand.
>
> O small white hands of children,
>   That seem of soft flower made!
> The ear of white to touch you
>   Bends, slightly swayed.
>
> Hands of poor little children,
>   Stretched out in hungry quest,
> Blessed are those that fill you,
>   Blessed and thrice blessed!
>
> Blessed those who hear you, seeming
>   A cry in their heart's core—
> Those who shall to the children
>   The world restore.

LITTLE FEET

> O tiny feet of children,
>   Blue with cold, unshod!
> How can they see, and not cover you—
>   O God!

> O little feet, sore wounded
>   By every stone and brier,
> Chilled by the songs in winter,
>   Defiled by mire!
>
> Man, blind, knows not where you go,
>   In valley or on height,
> You always leave behind a flower
>   Of living light.
>
> That where your little bleeding souls
>   You see, O childish feet!
> The tuberose in her snowy bloom
>   Becomes more sweet.
>
> Since in straight paths day after day
>   You travel bare,
> Be as heroic, little feet,
>   As you are fair.
>
> Two little suffering jewels,
>   Doomed to a bitter lot!
> How can the people pass you by
>   And see you not.

In a short prose sketch "To the Children," Gabriela addresses herself to the children whom she loved so much and to the memory she would like to leave with them as she writes:

> Many years hence, when I am a little heap of silent dust, play with me, with the earth of my heart and bones.
>
> If a mason gathers me up, he will make me into a brick, and I shall remain fast forever in a wall; but I have quiet niches. If they make me a brick in a prison, I shall grow red with shame when I hear a man sob; and if I am a brick in a school, I shall still suffer, because I cannot sing with you in the early mornings.
>
> I would rather be the dust with which you play, on the country roads. Clasp me, for I have been yours; unmake me, for I made you; trample upon me, because I did not give you the whole of beauty and the whole of truth. Only sing and run above me, so that I may kiss your beloved feet.

When you hold me in your hands, recite some beautiful verse; and I shall rustle with delight between your fingers. I shall rise up and look at you, seeking among you the eyes, the hair of those whom I have taught.

And when you make an image of me, break it every moment; for every moment the children broke me with tenderness and grief.

7

Turning Points

DEATH OF PETRONILA

The year 1929 was a decisive one in the evolution of Gabriela's religious faith. It was on the seventh of July that her beloved mother died in La Serena at the age of eighty-four.

Jorge Carrera Andrade and Cesar Arroyo brought her the news. They had received the telegram from Chile at the Consulate of Ecuador, where Gabriela had her postal address.

On being informed of Petronila's death, Gabriela's lips burst forth spontaneously in a moving expression of grief. Gabriela had always felt spiritually united with her mother, especially during her travels when she seemed to feel her unseen presence.

Although Gabriela had not lately expressed her belief in eternal life, the death of her mother reinforced her belief and dispelled any doubts she may have harbored. From her grief came the certainty of her belief in a future life.

The municipal authorities of La Serena participated in the funeral of her mother. After a religious ceremony in the Church of Saint Francis, her mother was buried in the cemetery there. Delegations from the Male High School, the High School for Girls, the Normal School, the School of the Mines, and the primary schools were present.

Gabriela never lost the sensation of her mother's presence and dedicated many of her most beautiful poems to her memory.

A SPOKESWOMAN FOR LATIN AMERICA

Gabriela continued working in the Institute of International Cooperation. She represented Chile in the International Congress of University Women, which met in Madrid.

In Bédarrides, Gabriela guided her friends in her talks on works of importance of Latin American writers. She discussed with them the destiny of America. She was concerned with the plight of José Vasconcelos and wished to form a group of "Friends of José Vasconcelos" to help him during his political exile. She also participated in the fight against racism and spoke frequently of her Basque and Indian origin.

New books arrived from all over Latin America. Those that she felt had literary or moral value found a pleasant place of honor in her house; others were disposed of in a dry well beneath her bedroom window. Andrade spoke of this:

> There was beneath the window of Gabriela's bedroom, a dry well that had been converted into a sepulcher and there in a small fire, bad books were burned to ashes in an exercise subjecting them to torture, black beetles, and little demons of the summer. The well of the books.[1]

GABRIELA'S PROSE

During this fertile period of her life, Gabriela wrote, besides poetry, beautiful works in prose. According to Luis Alberto Sanchez and Andrade, these articles were written in the finest prose of Latin America. Thus Gabriela restored its genre and ennobled it. Her love for the pure and primitive attracted her to medieval poetry. She approved a return to manual labor as a means of making a better world.

She wrote much about artisans and their works and about those who loved their works: Bernard Palissy, one of the creators of French ceramics in the seventeenth century; Frédéric Mistral, who, as a writer, was one of the founders of the Museum of Arts; Séverin, the apostle of justice; and many others.

In her article "The Perfumes of Grasse," Gabriela considered the cultivation of flowers to be one of the most beautiful tasks for women. She described with fervor violets, mimosas, roses, and acasias, revealing her love of nature and her deep knowledge of it. She identified herself with the women who worked the soil and recaptured the atmosphere of the countryside.

She wrote biographies of Saint Francis, Saint Theresa, Jean Marie Vianney, the rector of Ars, and other saints. Still living abroad, she wrote chronicles filled with poetry about her journeys in various countries. In 1930, she was living in Italy and called Florence "the most precious city in the world." She found Italy to be one of the most captivating countries, for she perceived the close bond that united the Italian people with those of Latin America.

UNITED STATES—1930

Toward the end of 1930, Gabriela made her second visit to the United States. She renewed her acquaintance with Professor de Onís, who had been responsible for getting her first book published at Columbia University, whose Barnard College invited her to give a course in Hispanic-American literature. She taught during the fall and spring semesters there.

She received a similar invitation from Vassar College where she remained until June. She enjoyed being with the students. Together they discussed everything under the sun. She was amazed at the youthful energy of the girls, their ease of manner, their independent character, frankness, and great curiosity about everything. Through her conversations with them, she became acquainted, firsthand, with the spirit of North American people.

In the summer of 1931, she occupied the chair of Hispanic-American literature in the School of Languages at Middlebury College in Vermont. Here she was impressed by the splendid elms and maples in Hepburn Hall park. Here on the shores of Lake Dunmore, the idyllic beauty of the Green Mountains brought peace to her nature-loving soul. The homelike atmosphere of the

Spanish-speaking department of the school captivated her. She would remember with nostalgia the nine months spent in that delightful retreat. She cherished the warm and friendly, yet somewhat reserved, manner of the people of New England.

Gabriela's pension had been suspended against the wishes of the Chilean president, Carlos Ibañez, and for a time she had to live on the income she received from her articles and classes. Yet she continued to be universally recognized.

While she was in New York, *Historiens chileans* appeared. This was the first volume of the *Ibero-American Collection*, translated into French by Georges Pillement with an introduction by Carlos Pereya. In Santiago de Chile, an article by Francisco Walker Linares on the League of Nations and Latin America revealed the important part Gabriela had played in preparing the *Ibero-American Collection*.

PUERTO RICO AND CENTRAL AMERICA

In 1931, Gabriela was asked to speak at the inauguration of a course in the University of Puerto Rico. She went there in July. During her stay on the island, she took the initiative in getting published a volume of the works of Eugenio María Hostos.

The Puerto Rican landscape impressed her deeply, and she loved it. This can be seen in her prose and poetry. She showed her love and concern for Puerto Rico by endeavoring to make it known to other lands that shared its language and culture. For over a decade she showed her interest through verses and numerous prose articles in the journal *Puerto Rico Illustrated* or in one of the Hispanic-American dailies: *El Mercurio* of Chile, *La Nación* of Buenos Aires, *El Universal* of Caracas, *El Tiempo* of Bogotá. These writings praised Puerto Rico and its people in an "impassioned, almost folkloric, deliberately disordered language."

Gabriela crossed the sea from Puerto Rico to visit the countries of Central America, where she was received with affection. In all parts, she spoke of the activities of the International Institute of Intellectual Cooperation and the *Ibero-American Collection*.

In a meeting with the president of Panama, she expressed the desire to include in the collection a volume of folklore of the country. Folklore had always been important for Gabriela and had been a part of her life since childhood.

With Alfonso Reyes, she wished to collect works of folklore from all Latin America. In a letter to Dominique Braga dated January 11, 1932, she wrote:

> I think it will be necessary to do much for the themes of American folklore and it will be very interesting to designate a volume for each country. It is the only original literature that we have.[2]

She proposed a second volume on the folklore of Chile.

BACK TO EUROPE AND CONSULAR SERVICE

In November, 1931, Gabriela took a trip to Germany with her friend Palma Guillén. In December, they went to Italy and stayed in Santa Margherita.

The year 1932 marked a new stage in Gabriela's life with her entry into the consular service. She was appointed consul by the Chilean authorities and assigned to the consulate at Naples. She worked at her new post for about three months, when she was refused approval by Mussolini because of anti-Fascist articles she had written, and she had to resign.

In March, 1932, she went to Paris to take part in the reunion of the Committee of Publications. While in France, she returned to Bédarrides, where she stayed for several months. In June, she visited Avignon, and in December, Lavagne, near Geneva, Switzerland. In January of 1933, she went to Barcelona.

PUERTO RICO AGAIN

In March, 1933, Gabriela returned to Puerto Rico where she stayed until June. She spoke at a number of conferences at the

University of Puerto Rico in Rio Piedras. There she helped form a committee with the object of securing the funds necessary to publish the volume with the works of de Hostos.

Gabriela taught a course in Hispanic literature at the University of Puerto Rico. There she delivered the Commencement Address and received the degree of Doctor Honoris Causa. The Puerto Rican legislature bestowed upon her the title, "adopted daughter of Puerto Rico."

SPAIN AGAIN

A little later, in July of 1933, Gabriela went back to Spain. There, in Madrid, she was named Honorary Consul, to replace Victor Domingo Silva. She received no salary and lived on what she received from periodical articles published in Spain and Latin America, and honorariums received for courses she taught in Puerto Rico and the United States. During her residence in Spain, Gabriela visited Barcelona, and Málaga, among other places. In Málaga she chaired a conference whose theme was *"A Brief Description of Chile"*; her lecture was published in Santiago by the University of Chile Press. A series of poems, with the title *White Clouds,* saw light that same year. Gabriela was well known in Spain as a writer and for her collaboration with the Spanish press and her great generosity.

While she was consul in Madrid, Gabriela discovered the language that her mother had spoken. She blended in certain archaic expressions that were used by men in Spanish literature. Gabriela would say with a smile, "I speak a blended language." At the same time she referred to Spain as "the mother country."

Gabriela had conflicting feelings about Spain. On one hand, she recalled the evils of the conquest and the mistreatment of the Indians in the Spanish *encomiendas*. Against this she weighed her feelings of affection for the Spanish people in the midst of their afflictions.

Gabriela did not close her eyes to the problems facing Spain, but she considered them realistically, as she had in Latin America in her struggle to raise the level of life of the common people.

She did not love Spain as a stranger, but as a daughter familiar with its writers and particularly its mystics. She had traveled all through Spain and was familiar with all its regions, but she felt closest to the Basque people whose blood she carried in her veins.

In her first visit to Spain in 1925, on crossing Castile, she had written a moving article on Saint Teresa Ávila. She imagined that the saint was with her and had helped her to understand that part of Spain. She felt the saint had guided her with love and that they talked about the similarities and differences between Spain and Latin America.

Gabriela collaborated in local periodicals, especially *ABC* and the *Sun* of Madrid. These articles, which were also published in Latin America, reflected her admiration and respect for many Spanish writers; they showed her understanding of what she felt the country was really like. Among the titles were "Enrique Diez," "Unamuno," "Lope," "Remarks about Cataluna," and "Remarks about an Anthology of don Federico de Onís."

CONSUL FOR LIFE

In August, 1935, a group of European writers, including Miguel de Unamuno, Guglielmo Ferrero, Romain Rolland, George Duhamel, and Maurice Maeterlinck, sent a petition to the then president of Chile, Arturo Alessandri Palma, in which they asked that Gabriela be given the post of consul with a salary that would provide her with an appropriate amount of security. The request was approved with the help of the president and the home minister, Gustavo Rossi. The congress passed a special law, which was put in effect by the president on September 17, 1935. The law created for Gabriela the post of Consul for Life.

In October, 1935, Gabriela was transferred to Lisbon with the grade of Consul of the Second Class. There she began to appreciate the richness of Portuguese literature and to learn that soft and beautiful language.

Again, here in Lisbon, Gabriela converted the consulate into a place of refuge for all who needed help and asked for it.

Adelaida Portillo spoke of the manner in which she was received in Gabriela's social circle with these words:

> I arrived in Lisbon absolutely demoralized. I knew that Gabriela Mistral was there as Consul, and without knowing her, called at her door. She provided me a place of refuge and the magic circle closed around me from that moment. To her I owe the recovery of my equilibrium, . . . Gabriela was attractive as a light and protector of a home. For me, to speak of Gabriela, is to speak of the delta of a river.[3]

Gabriela's house was open to her friends or to strangers who needed help. With them she would spend hours of conversation after a frugal meal. The talk would consist of discussion of various themes, anecdotes, Chilean narratives, and folklore. These conversations, engraved upon those present, formed a work of art that synthesized her ideal of beauty and reality.

Victor Andres Belaunde, later president of the General Assembly of the United Nations, compared the conversations with perfume.

CHILEAN FOLKLORE PROJECT

On November 25, 1936, Gabriela went to Paris to assist in a meeting of the Committee of Publication for the Collection. She proposed the formation of a subcommittee to collect materials for the volume of Chilean folklore.

In February, 1937, while she was back in Lisbon she received notice of her appointment to the Committee of Arts and Literature and of a coming *entretien* to be held in Paris.

Gabriela had just returned from a long trip through France, Germany, and Denmark. In Copenhagen she had stayed with Palma Guillén, who represented her country as Minister Plenipotentiary in 1937-1938.

Gabriela took part in the *entretien* in July of 1937. The theme of the conference was "The Future of Literature." Gabriela spoke of the economic situation of the American writer and the hard road the poet had to travel. She spoke of her desire to help.

At the end of August, 1937, Gabriela left for Brazil, a trip she had planned since 1936. In Saó Paulo she was declared an honorary member of the Pan-American Society of Brazil for her great effort as the "priestess of American sisterhood."

From Brazil, Gabriela went to Argentina, where she felt united with the people because of her Argentinian mother. She said:

> "There is a quality of light in our Cordilleras of which I am reminded hearing these sisters, a light that was sweet, bright. I signed with pleasure and happiness the registers of the Argentinian Union of Women to accept the good influence zone so special to our America.[4]

She sent to Dominique Braga the preface she had decided to write for the volume *Folklore Chilean,* translated by Georgette and Jacques Soustelle and published in July, 1938, through the auspices of the International Institute of Intellectual Cooperation. In this work she described with realism the customs of the Auraucanian Indians and revealed how much she understood them. To her, the book was more than a collection of works of folklore filled with color. It was a medium through which European writers could understand the life and thought of the Chilean Indians and their love for the mountains and the sea.

While Gabriela was in Buenos Aires, Victoria Ocampo invited her to spend a few weeks at her home at the Mar del Plata. As was her custom, after a frugal meal, Gabriela spent many happy hours, seated and smoking one cigarette after another and speaking without pause. The children made her happy, and the son of the gardener was for her an agreeable companion.

Gabriela spent many happy and carefree days in the country home of Victoria. She stayed there until the seventh of April, when the pair observed their joint birthdays together. To celebrate the coincidence, Gabriela dedicated a poem, "Compliments to Victoria Ocampo in the Argentine." She praised her friend, her country, the beauty of the land, and the defense of liberty in America.

TALA

Gabriela's third book of verses, *Tala* (Felling), appeared in 1938. To understand it, we must remember that it was a compilation of poems written at different times under diverse circumstances. In the space of years from 1922 to 1938, Gabriela's life and art had undergone profound changes.

During those sixteen years after *Desolation* had been published, no book by Gabriela, except *Tenderness,* had appeared, although during that time, she had been published in the newspapers and periodicals of Hispanic America. Despite what some thought, her voice had not been silent. Proof of her continued work and the steps she had taken to perfect her art can be found in the pages of newspapers through those years, among which are *El Repertorio Americano* of Costa Rica, *El Tiempo* of Colombia, *La Nación* and *Critica* of Buenos Aires, and the journals *Atenea, Sur* and *Bimestre Cubana,* besides what was published in Spain and translated in the dailies of France, Portugal, and Brazil.

Like *Desolation, Felling* was born of a particular set of circumstances. It came as a gesture of love, a generous act of charity toward the children of Spain, innocent victims scattered to the four corners of the earth during the Spanish Civil War.

Gabriela was both ashamed and astonished at the indifference in the Americas to the plight of the children; she believed that they should have been the first to receive the children of Spanish blood. It is significant that Mexico was the only American land whose moral attitude toward the dilemma of the helpless Spanish children proved the exception to the indifference that shocked Gabriela.

The manuscript of *Felling* was offered as a gift to the children of Spain—the Catalonians, Castilians, and Basques—who had been uprooted from their homes by the foreign invasion. Proceeds from sales went to the children's camp of Pedralles and also helped to alleviate the poverty of the concentration camps in France. The prestige of the poetess guaranteed successful sales and a high profit. The book was dedicated to her friend, Palma Guillén.

The book's title, *Felling,* refers to the felling of trees, which established the nature of its contents. The poems were offered as fragments that had been cut from a living body that still retains its stumps and roots. According to Miss Arce:

> The action of creation is seen as a release, and deep within the mutilated trunks, there remains the latent promise of a new forest.[5]

At the end of the book, Gabriela offers some notes in which she defends the right to say something about her own work to help the reader "like an elf that suddenly appears before him and walks with him along the road a bit." There are notes of personal confession, the religious crisis provoked by her mother's death, the rediscovery of hope, and the negative appraisal of sorrow.

Her mother's presence was never to leave Gabriela. In the first section, the poem "Death of My Mother" establishes the continuity between *Desolation* and *Felling.*

> Oh mother, in my dreams
> I walk through tortuous landscapes.
> I climb a dark mountain
> beyond which there always outlined another,
> where undefined you stand,
> and there is still another mountain to overcome
> to make my way
> to the mountain of my rejoicing with you.

This section includes "The Flight," "Nocturnes of Consummation," "The Defeat," and "Old Weavers," which prolong her spiritual crisis mentioned before. Then come those poems that manifest a return of hope as a true entry in a new moral climate. These include "Mad Litanies" and "Nocturne of the Descent." The first sings of the joy of faith in resurrection, where the pain of her mother's death transforms itself into the certainty of a future life in the peace of Christ. This profound change occurred

Turning Points

after she had read Henri Bergson on Christian mysticism; it moved Gabriela deeply and started her longing and searching for grace.

The second section, "Hallucination," contains poems of recollections, dreams, and visions, like "Paradise," "Midnight," and "Tales of the Madwoman." These poems gather together the major elements of Gabriela's latest poetry—death, the absolute, poetry and dreams. They are tales of a madwoman, but contain some of the deepest and most elaborate thoughts of the poetess.

Other sections include "Matter," "Creatures," "Messages," "America." "Joy," "Lullabies," and "The Story World." These parts contain five fundamental themes—religious crisis, evocation of the past, self-confession, children, beings, and nature.

8

The Nobel Prize

CUBA

In the summer of 1938, Gabriela visited Havana, Cuba, where she was acknowledged as an apostle whose mission it was to unify the American intellectual world. In a discourse there on one occasion, she said that she divided the world into three categories: countries of the Father that were strong, brusque; countries of the Son that were gentle; and countries of the Holy Spirit that were vehement and violent. She placed Mexico and Cuba in the last category. Chile, she felt, belonged in the first. Gabriela declared:

> I believe that Chile is the daughter of God the Father. We are strong, at times somewhat brusque, and then sorrowful or repentant. The grace of the Holy Spirit does not shower upon us, or of late upon us.[1]

Another time she spoke of the popular Cuban music that had been her company in Europe where she had listened to Cuban records.

On October 30, 1938, she gave a talk on *Versos secillas* of the Cuban hero and poet, José Martí.

A CONSUL'S LIFE

Later in the year, Gabriela returned to Europe and was appointed consul at Nice. While there, plans were made to combine in one volume the French version of some of her works in prose and verse. Mathilde Pomés translated the poems and Francis de Momandre the selections in prose. They were planning to send the manuscript to the editor on the first of July, 1940, but the Second World War interrupted the project. Mathilde Pomés had just completed the translation of the poems during the bombardment of Paris.

In 1940, Gabriela was transferred to Brazil at her request. She wished above all to watch over and protect Juan Miguel, her beloved nephew.

Gabriela was first assigned as consul in Niterol. Then in 1941 she went to Petrópolis. This was a picturesque mountain city with an altitude of eight hundred meters. It was only about seventy-five kilometers from Rio de Janeiro, the capital, to which Gabriela made brief visits.

Gabriela met Dominique Braga, her friend and colleague from the now defunct International Institute of Intellectual Cooperation, who had been transferred to Brazil during the war. He invited Gabriela to visit his new home, which had been the home of the Count Francisco de Figueredo, Dominique's maternal grandfather.

Gabriela continued collaborating with the principal dailies of Latin America. She took an active part in the cause of the Allies. She kept up a correspondence with her "godsons of war," Brazilian soldiers who fought in Europe. She spoke out against Fascism. She condemned the hate and oppression of the Jews. She displayed untiring efforts to awaken spirituality over all of Brazil and the countries where Spanish was spoken.

Gabriela was never alone, for she would see people in all spheres of human activity. At one time, her friend Hortensia de Rio Branco, daughter of the former minister of Exterior Relations of Brazil, lived in her home. Also, taking refuge there, was the French actress Falconetti of the French comedy, and her small daughter.

Among her friends, besides Dominique Braga, who was the founder of the French Alliance in Petrópolis, were Fedor Ganz, literary mentor of Yin-Yin, her nephew, and many prominent Brazilian writers. Gabriela was also close friends with Stefan Zweig, the Austrian writer in exile in Brazil, and his wife.

In essence, Gabriela gathered a small court around her, though humble, where she reigned a sovereign. In a discussion of literature, she moved with a majestic air.

Always championing the cultivation and dissemination of folklore, in February, 1941, Gabriela wrote a prologue for the book, *Chile o una loca geografia,* by Benjamin Supercaseaux, published by Ediciones Ercilla in Santiago in 1942. In it the poetess expressed her gratitude to the author because he expressed his love for folklore and his native soil.

TWO TRAGEDIES

On February 23, 1942, Stefan Zweig, having become discouraged at the condition he found in the world and the destiny of the Jewish people, committed suicide along with his young wife. He was sixty-one, and she was thirty-three. This unexpected tragedy cast deep grief on Gabriela and her friends. Back in 1935, Gabriela had condemned the persecution of the Hebrew people and would defend their cause all her life.

The Zweigs had lived for a time in one of the rooms of Gabriela's house. At the time of their deaths, they were living just a few blocks away.

Zweig had considered Gabriela an expert on plants as he had seen the tender care with which she cultivated her garden. Both shared a love for rural life.

The tragedy of the war years, so discouraging, and the suicide of her friends, were not the only blows Gabriela was to receive. A personal tragedy overwhelmed her on the fourteenth of August, 1943, with the death of her nephew, Juan Miguel.

Yin-Yin, as he was called, was a boy—very intelligent and capricious—with a talent for writing; he had received a French education. Fedor Ganz, who had taught him Latin, said that he showed an inclination toward the humanities. Gabriela, as a part of his education, instilled in him a love of nature and hoped that he would live a rural life and study the science of agriculture. Through 1943, Juan had been raised largely among adults. He was now an adolescent of seventeen with great sensibility. He had shared the wandering life of Gabriela since he was four years old. He considered Palma Guillén, with whom he had lived on occasion for several months at a time, a great friend, his second mother, to whose counsel he listened.

The young man felt very close to Gabriela, whom he called "Buda," and, as she wished, accompanied her on her walks. He remained at her side when she was sick. He read to her and enriched her spirit with juvenile talk.

This nephew was for Gabriela more than a part of her life; he was her life, and his death was a heavy blow to her whole being. It enfeebled her spirit and her will to live.

For seven days, Gabriela was incapable of moving, and for some time remained in a state of prostration. She wanted desperately to see him in her dreams and in her waking hours. The days seemed to run into each other without change in condition or color.

The cause of Juan Miguel's death was in part a mystery, but this much is known. It was not a natural death. He was influenced to take arsenic through the cruelty of school companions who had made his life unbearable. Because Juan had studied in Europe, the boys showed an antipathy toward him and looked on him as a stranger. To them, he appeared an international figure belonging to a higher class. They envied and hated him because of his cordiality and generous personality.

Juan was a deeply sensitive boy, who may have been excessively impressed by the suicide of the Zweigs in 1942. The double suicide, just a few houses away, had affected the boy as deeply as it had Gabriela.

In a farewell note to Gabriela, Juan Miguel wrote, "Mama, pardon. It is better to kill oneself, than to kill." He died five hours later in a hospital. Although he struggled for his life, he accepted death with stoicism.

Gabriela remained at his side during his suffering. She wrote:

> Ay, but I have to return to my old heresy and to believe in Karma of past lives, to understand the transgressions for which I have been punished with the night of agony of my Juan Miguel in a hospital, to think of the incredible stoicism as he bore the sharp pains of agony in his poor, beloved body.[2]

Palma Guillén came immediately to Gabriela's assistance. She remained with her during the period from 1943 to 1945. These two years were the saddest of Gabriela's life.

The cause of Juan Miguel's death was clouded because Gabriela insisted that he had been assassinated. The police certified that it was caused by self-inflicted arsenic poisoning. People closest to Gabriela, her secretaries, testified to the boy's suicide. They felt he had killed himself because he had failed to adapt to the Portuguese language; Brazilian law required him to repeat work he had already done in France.

The Brazilian poet Manuel Bandeira thought a deformity of the spine may have caused a nervous condition that finally led to self-destruction.

Gabriela herself may have unwittingly hurt him at a particularly vulnerable period. Her adverse comment on a novel the boy had written shattered his self-esteem and caused him to tear up the manuscript. Moreover, Juan Miguel had called her "Buda" because of her cold and rigid insistence on righteousness and purity.

Despite obvious evidence to the contrary, Gabriela insisted that the boy had enjoyed a good physical and emotional health. Thus he could have no reason for suicide. According to Gabriela, another youth had reported to her that a gang of young neo-Nazis, called "Bocdades," had taunted Juan Miguel because he refused to join them. They taunted him because of his white skin, his wealth, and the reputation of his family. Finally, they said he was a bastard.

Gabriela said that the school Juan attended had mostly Negroes and mulattos, many of whom were antagonistic to the few whites who were there. Juan would come home covered with bruises from blows that they had given him. They resented his being surrounded by comforts that they did not have. For this, the gang made him an object of torment. Gabriela felt that they had brought on his death; that they had killed him, because they couldn't forgive him for possessing so much that they did not have.

GABRIELA'S HEALTH

Gabriela's health had a part in her own attitude toward life, death, and suffering. Her problems with diabetes had not been diagnosed until 1930; it had brought her to the edge of serious illness many times before.

Because of her physical disabilities, Gabriela needed a traveling companion to look after her meals, medicines, and general well-being. Back in 1922, she had not been able to remain in Mexico City for long periods of time because of the high altitude and had to participate in the administrative duties of the schools and library system from the coastal area. She moved about constantly, not just to escape boredom, but to achieve spiritual satisfaction and respite from physical ailments.

THE NOBEL PRIZE

While Gabriela lived her personal tragedy, peace again shone down upon the world. With that peace, the eyes of Stockholm were again focused on Chile. In 1938, a movement had been started to present her as a candidate from all Latin America for the Nobel Prize, although, according to the critic Norberto Pinella, the idea of presenting Gabriela Mistral for the Nobel Prize belongs to Virgilio Figuera, author of *La divina Gabriela,* first biography of the poetess which was published in 1933. Again, in 1941, an article by Ivan Harrie, critic for a daily newspaper in Stockholm, Sweden, appeared in *El Mercurio* which said that Gabriela Mistral might very well be chosen for the Nobel Prize. Harrie had written:

> It is possible that when there is peace again in the world, the Nobel Prize will go to Chile. In that case one of the "eighteen" has made a sensational discovery in contemporary literature: the poetess Gabriela Mistral, who is presented in *Bouniers Littera Magacin* with a few verses, translated, and comments by Hjalmar Guilberg.[3]

In 1942, at the initiative of the Carioca Academy of Letters, an article was published in various parts of Central America that suggested the Nobel Prize ought to go to Gabriela Mistral. But the world was in the midst of the horrors of war and awarding of the Nobel Prize was suspended.

Now, with the war over, the time was right for the poetry and prose of a woman who had sung of love for the weak and oppressed and of her desire and eagerness for social justice.

On the fifteenth of November, 1945, the telephone of Gabriela Mistral in Petrópolis rang constantly. She was being awarded the Nobel Prize for Literature. When she heard the news over the radio, Gabriela knelt down before the crucifix, which was always near, and thanked God for the high honor that had been bestowed upon her.

When the minister of Sweden in Brazil informed her of the award, she said, "I am grateful for the honor which Hispanic-American literature receives."

The first Nobel Prize for Literature awarded to a Latin American went to Gabriela Mistral, the voice of Chile.

Among the women who had previously received the Nobel Prize were the Norwegian writer Selma Lagerlöf, who had been compared with Gabriela; Sigrid Undset, the Norwegian novelist; Madame Curie, Grazzia Deledda, and Pearl Buck.

The Spanish novelist Jacinto Benavente, who had received the Prize in 1922, spoke of the recognition of the value of the work of the poetess:

> Gabriela merits it as few have. The name of Gabriela already is consecrated through her singular work in teaching and her poetry so earthy and feminine. We are all grateful for this new triumph of our literature.[4]

Much earlier Maria Monvel had written:

> Unsurpassed, absolute, complete, multiple, Gabriela Mistral is the greatest poetess America has produced and the greatest of all times in the Spanish language.[5]

Augusto Iglesias wrote that throughout the Spanish world, thousands of women see, with justification, the renaissance of the indigenous race of America in the triumph of Gabriela.

> Thousands of women in hundreds of colleges in native America see in her triumph something of a Renaissance of the race.[6]

On the eighteenth of November, 1945, Gabriela Mistral, accompanied by Maria Terra, wife of the nephew of ex-President Terra of Uruguay, sailed for Stockholm on the Swedish steamship *Ecuator*; she was in very poor health. The Swedish press said of Gabriela on her arrival:

> She has exactly the aspect that a poetess-laureate for the Nobel Prize ought to have. She is tall, well-built, imposing and superior. . . . Her face is a true reflection of the bare truth, that which is expressed in her poetry.[7]

On December 10, 1945, in the Philharmonic Palace, Gabriela Mistral received the Nobel Prize for Literature from the hands of King Gustaf. She advanced with due solemnity, in a shining black velvet dress. Her majestic carriage gave her a queenly appearance.

Hjalmar Guilberg, a member of the Swedish Academy and translator of some of Gabriela's poetry, gave a short address. In a few words, he reviewed the story and legend of the "spiritual queen of all Latin America." Hjalmar Guilberg spoke to the assembled people:

> Gabriela shared her maternal love with the children whom she taught. It was for them that she wrote those simple sounds and rounds collected in Madrid in 1924 under the title of

Ternura (Tenderness). Once in her honor, four thousand Mexican children sang her rounds. Gabriela Mistral became the poet of motherhood by adoption.

It was not until 1938, in Buenos Aires, that for the benefit of the young victims of the Spanish Civil War, her third great collection, *Tala (Felling)*, appeared—a title that might be translated as "devastation" but which also means a game. In contrast with the pathetic mood of *Desolación*, *Tala* exhales the cosmic calm that envelops the South American earth whose perfume reaches unto us. We find ourselves anew in the garden, to hear her intimate conversation with nature and with things. Through a curious mixture of holy hymns and naïve songs for children, of poems about bread and wine, salt, wheat, water—this water that one might very bend to the needs of thirsty men—sing the primitive needs of life.

From her maternal hand this poet offers her portion, which has the savor of earth and which quenches the thirst of the heart. It is part of that source that flowed from the Isles of Greece for Sappho, and for Gabriela Mistral in the valley of Elqui, the source of poetry that never dries up on the earth.[8]

Then the Swedish Academy member spoke directly to the Chilean poetess:

Gabriela Mistral, you have made a very long voyage in order to hear so short a speech. Within a few minutes, I have related for the countrymen of Selma Lagerlöf, as if it were a story, the amazing journey that has taken you from the desk of schoolmistress to the throne of poetry. It is to render homage to the riches of South American literature that we address ourselves today, especially to its queen, the poet of *Desolación*, who has become the great singer of mercy and motherhood. From the hands of His Royal Majesty, I beg you to receive the Nobel Prize for Literature which the Swedish Academy awards you.[9]

In her reply, Gabriela displayed a spirit identified with the American continent. She spoke not in her own name but in the name of the Latin American nations, as she said:

Today, Sweden has turned to Latin America to honor one of the many works of its culture. The universal spirit of Alfred

> Nobel was pleased to include in its radius the preservation of the cultural life of the southern hemisphere of the American continent so little and so badly known.
>
> Through a fortune that overwhelms me, I am the voice of the poets of my race and indirectly that of the noble language of Spanish and Portuguese. Both are happy to have been invited to become acquainted with nordic life, and all her assistance through her folklore and her poetry.[10]

After the ceremony, Gabriela explained that she had not been nervous on receiving the Nobel Prize because her thoughts were on her dead nephew, whom she had loved as a son.

Gabriela remained in Sweden for a month. All the institutions and organizations representing the country paid homage to her. She won the hearts of the Swedish people as they had won hers. They looked upon her as another Selma Lagerlöf. She was invited to stay as long as she liked.

It was reported by *Time* magazine that Gabriela was the "lioness of social Stockholm." As a result of her visit to Sweden, Gabriela considered that country's social democracy to be a century ahead of everything else.

EUROPEAN VISIT

After leaving Sweden, Gabriela visited France, Italy, and Great Britain, countries that she had been to before the war. Although her health was bad, she traveled alone.

In Paris, Gabriela was met at the airport and made an official guest of the government. The Ministry of Foreign Relations named Mathilda Pomés to accompany her to many ceremonies and entertainments held in her honor. She was surrounded by personal friends and writers.

The book of Gabriela's poems that had been translated into French before the war finally appeared in 1946. The same year, another book of translations by her good friend, Roger Caillois, was published in France.

In Italy, Gabriela received an honorary doctoral degree from the University of Florence.

While in Rome, Gabriela was granted a beautiful private audience with Pope Pius XII. She learned that he was acquainted with the brilliance of Buenos Aires, gigantic and European, but that he knew little of the material and spiritual plight of the millions of neglected Indians living at or below the poverty level. She asked the Pope for nothing for herself but for the help for Indians of America who were her brothers. It was an hour of friendship that was engraved in an unforgettable memory after she left his presence.

It was sometime later that Gabriela read with pleasure that the Pope had initiated a campaign to help reach the Indians of South America.

DORIS DANA

After spending some time in England early in 1946, Gabriela left Europe for the United States.

At a conference at Barnard College in New York, she met Doris Dana for the first time. Miss Dana was a great admirer of Thomas Mann, the German philosopher and writer. She had been asked to translate an article by Gabriela, "The Other Unfortunate German," for a book about Mann. Thus, indirectly, the German writer became the means of drawing the two women together. Doris Dana became a close and beloved friend of Gabriela and later would be designated as her literary heir.

WHITE HOUSE RECEPTION

In January, 1946, the press reported that Gabriela's countrymen were planning to make her Chilean birthplace a cultural center. Many schools and libraries in Latin America had already been named in her honor. The following March, Gabriela was received at the White House by President Harry Truman.

The United States, she felt, had the strongest pulse of life and creation. She praised the qualities of American men, and had the highest kind of admiration for American women. During her stay in Washington, the Union of American Women conferred upon her the title of "Woman of the Americas." She was also feted in other cities.

UNITED NATIONS DELEGATE

Gabriela had been a delegate from Chile to the United Nations Commission on the Juridical and Social Conditions of Women. After attending some meetings, she resigned in May, 1946. One of the reasons for her action was disagreement with the aims of the subcommittee. She did not believe that the way for women to obtain equal rights with men was through special protective legislation; she felt that this procedure would not equalize but, rather, lower the status of women. Common legislation on the other hand, would raise women's status, making it equal to that of men. Gabriela declared that she was not a fighter or an official feminist.

9
Failing Health

CALIFORNIA

Gabriela was named by her country as consul in Los Angeles, a position she held until 1948. For a while she lived in Monrovia near Pasadena. Her state of health was deteriorating and she suffered from arteriosclerosis, as well as diabetes; for a time she was almost blind.

Although she was ill and depressed, she continued to receive visitors from both North and South America—friends, writers, artists, and professors. Her friendship with Doris Dana continued to grow.

Gabriela was not too happy with the climate and conditions in Monrovia. After a year, she bought a small house at 729 Anapanu Street in Santa Barbara. Here she found some relaxation in the countryside. Her new home, more to her liking, was surrounded by trees, one of which was more than a hundred years old. Later, when she was in Italy, she would write to friends in Santa Barbara asking them to look after that tree, which was more important to her than the house. She wrote:

> All I have is a house with two or three thousand books, in California, and with a tree more than one hundred years old. I write that you may take care of that tree.[1]

Many of the poems that were written in Santa Barbara would appear later in *Wine Press* (Lagar), her final book.

Failing Health

The University of California at Los Angeles and Mills College in Oakland awarded Gabriela doctoral degrees. She went personally to accept them and also visited Berkeley, San Diego, Long Beach, Pasadena, and Ojai.

From California, Gabriela continued her correspondence with Don Zacarías Gomez in Chile. In a letter dated October 3, 1947, she again showed interest in the Rosicrucians. She thanked him for having sent her a copy of *Revista Teosófica* that contained articles by Pearl Buck and Ramon Clares. The correspondence showed Gabriela's continued interest in theosophy, the Rosicrucians, meditation, the occult, and healing through concentration, prayer, and proper diet.

Don Zacarías had willingly undertaken the management of Gabriela's personal and business matters during the time that she was abroad. The job offered no salary nor did it take constant attention to handle her financial affairs. But whenever she needed specific help, Don Zacarías was the trusted friend she turned to. This might be distributing money to the poor, sending a check to her half-sister, Emelina, or finding out why checks she had coming had not arrived.

It was Zacarías who telegraphed her the news of Emelina's death on March 28, 1947.

MEXICO REVISITED

In 1948, when Gabriela was suffering greatly from diabetes, she was invited by the Mexican president to come to Mexico for her health.

When she arrived in Yucatan, her sickness grew worse and she was at the point of death. She later wrote:

> My collapse in Yucatan lasted three hours. An American doctor saved me and explained that the triple injection used in desperation left my heart worse than before.[2]

For a time she felt herself a prisoner in her home. Because of her heart trouble, she could not go to Mexico City or fulfill her desire to see the school at San Angel, where she had once had peace and happiness.

She lived for a time in Mérida in the state of Yucatan and at various places in Veracruz. She stayed on some farms near a village where there were some Indians whom she loved so much.

Gabriela had come to Mexico as the guest of President Alemán, his wife, dona Beatriz Velasco de Alemán, and the poet Jaime Torres Bodet, then director of UNESCO (United Nations Educational, Scientific, and Cultural Organization). She had intended to stay from three to six months, but remained there for about two years as consul at Veracruz. She gave many conferences and dedicated her time to the people in the villages who needed her help and understanding, and to writing.

MORE TRAVEL

In 1950, Gabriela returned to the United States. On the twelfth of December, she visited the Congressional Library in Washington with some of her poems, and while in the city, she received special recognition from the North American Academy of Franciscan History.

A little later, Gabriela was named consul in Italy. She lived in Rapallo, in a little house close to the sea and surrounded by trees.

Later, when she was consul in Naples, she lived at 220 la via Tasso. Her home attracted many Latin American visitors. She worked as a consultant for UNESCO. She was offered the directorship of the South American Fund of the United Nations International Children's Emergency Fund (UNICEF), but was unable to accept because of delicate health. Although Gabriela was not the official founder of UNICEF, she was considered its spiritual founder, and had made the first call to the world in favor of this work. Always involved in charitable work, she was named honorary president of an organization established in Rome, born as a consequence of the invasion. It was presided over by Raul Villedieu, general secretary of the Franciscan Academy in Rome.

Failing Health

When Gabriela was consul in Naples, her friend, Palma Guillén, was engaged in a special mission in Rome. They came together for eight- or ten-day periods several times. Palma would help to select a work of prose and type it to be sent to some review or a friend. From time to time, Palma would discover some excellent verse in some forgotten corner.

In 1953, the Cuban government invited Gabriela to participate in the centennial celebration honoring José Martí. She was on this trip accompanied by a North American friend, Margaret Bates, with whom she had become acquainted in Rome. Gabriela had given her the nickname "Daughter of Rome." In Havana, they stayed at the home of the Cuban writer Dulce Maria Loynaz. The Cubans were acknowledging their debt to Martí for the verses and articles he had written about Cuba.

On her return from Cuba, Gabriela spent a month in Florida and then went to New York, where she represented Chile as a delegate in the seventh session of the Commission of the Juridical and Social Condition of the Woman in the United Nations. The session lasted from March 16 to April 3, 1953. She also attended the eighth session from March 22 to April 9, 1954.

Gabriela lived briefly in New York City and then went to the home of Doris Dana in Roslyn Harbor on Long Island. This beautiful home was surrounded by flowers and the view through the window was most pleasant for the Chilean poetess.

In 1954, Gabriela traveled to the University of New Orleans, where she chaired a series of conferences.

She also went to Pittsburgh, where she participated in a fiesta for writers organized by Pedro Juan Labarthe. Here she read parts of her "Poema de Chile."

RETURN TO CHILE

Among the concerns that Gabriela had, revealed in various conversations, were the social conditions of women and children in Chile, the problems of education, and an effort to help the young writers of her country. She liked to help young writers discover the significance of poetry and selected basic themes for her lectures. Her only luxury was the purchase of a great number of books which she shared with her friends, young and old. She spoke, for example, of the merits of the Greek classics and the literary works of the Italians, especially Dante, whom she called with affection, "My father Dante."

She had for many years during her absence from Chile sent money, books, and clothing to the children of her beloved Valley of Elqui, which helped her feel near to them. She sent them many worthwhile books through her Spanish friend Pedro Moral, to help enrich the stock of the library at Vicuña, which was named after her.

As evidence of her devotion to the children, when she received the National Prize of Literature in Chile in 1951, she asked that the value be distributed in her name among the children of her native valley.

In August, 1954, Gabriela embarked on the steamship *Santa Maria* for Chile. With her was Doris Dana. She was again in her native country on the fifth of September after sixteen years of absence. She had made the trip at the invitation of the president of Chile, General Carlos Ibañez, on behalf of his government. Two days before they arrived, the Editorial del Pacifico of Santiago had published a new edition of *Desolación*.

The welcome she received in all parts was moving. She disembarked in Valparaíso, the chief port of Chile and one of the cities that she liked best. A special train awaited to carry her in triumph to the capital at Santiago.

Thousands of children, women, teachers, workers, young people and old, waited at each stop of the train—Viña del Mar, Limache, Quillota, La Calera—to see her, singing at times some of the poems that had been set to music.

From the window of her railway car, Gabriela waved her hand to the children and said with emotion: "How good and beautiful to see the children of my land. I will come again to see them and talk with them. I will visit them in their schools and in their homes."[3]

Greeted by dignitaries on the platform in Santiago, Gabriela expressed her happiness to be again in Chile: "I am happy, very happy, to set foot again on Chilean soil. One of my best dreams that I now see realized, was this, of going to Santiago to be again with mine, with you."[4]

Gabriela was taken by automobile to the Palacio de la Moneda. Thousands of persons watched her pass by along the principal artery of Santiago. Gabriela went through the arch of triumph with its inscription, "The good sower scatters her songs." The children sang their childhood rounds. Students from the secondary schools were present and scattered flowers across her route.

On being presented to the people who had gathered to honor and hear her, Gabriela spoke of the pleasure it gave her to talk to the people, the workers, and the country folk. She spoke in an intimate tone as an old teacher talking to her children.

Gabriela received an honorary doctoral degree on September 10, 1954. In her acceptance speech, she referred to the intellectual mission of the teacher whose desire ought to be more than specific obligations to help the needy and to unite spiritually the people of the city and the countryside. Gabriela had read only the first part of her discourse when she discovered that she had left the rest of her notes at home. She then improvised for about an hour or more to the general public as if talking to a few intimate friends. She spoke of her impressions of the various European countries— Italy, Belgium, and Denmark—of her deep interest in making better the economic and cultural conditions of the people of the countryside. She recalled anecdotes from her life in the various regions of Chile, and the particular regard she had for those in Punta Arenas in the extreme south of Chile. She spoke of the future of the country, the need for agrarian reform, and the struggle to combat poverty, and asked her hearers to consider the condition of the miners whose cause she had always defended.

Doris Dana had to interrupt her when an hour had passed because Gabriela, in her preoccupation with the welfare of the people, had forgotten the time and might have gone on indefinitely.

In the Presidential Palace, Gabriela was received by President Ibañez and other high officials.

Gabriela remained in Chile for more than a month and received many honors. Most impressive was the gathering of forty thousand children in the National Stadium to see and hear her and sing her songs.

RETURN TO THE UNITED STATES

In October, 1954, Gabriela returned to the United States. At the end of that month she received an honorary doctoral degree from Columbia University in New York. The occasion was the bicentennial of that institution of higher learning. Among the forty-eight persons who were honored at the same time were the Queen Mother of Great Britain, Adlai Stevenson, Konrad Adenauer, and Dag Hammerskjöld.

From that time on until her death, Gabriela lived in the home of Doris Dana in Roslyn Harbor on Long Island.

LAGAR

In December, 1954, the Editorial de Pacifico of Santiago published her new book, *Lagar* (Wine Press). It was an expression of gratitude for the cordial and vibrant welcome she had received from the people of Chile, the only thing that she could give them.

It was sixteen years after *Tala* (Felling) that Gabriel had the Chilean firm publish *Lagar* (Wine Press)—her swan song. The book omitted much of what she had written during those turbulent sixteen years; it was more of a mirror of her personal life and suffering.

Doris Dana recalled the effect of those years on Gabriela, her beloved friend. They were cruel years. She had not been able to "leave behind the dark ravine and climb up gentler slopes" as she had hoped. She had observed the Spanish Civil War and all its terrible atrocities. Her book *Tala* (Felling) had been published for the benefit of children displaced during the conflict among the

Spanish peoples. She had seen the black clouds of fascism darken the European skies after their direct interference in the struggle in Spain. She had observed with horror the holocaust of another World War. She had endured many personal sorrows, the deaths of many close friends, including Stefan Zweig, the death of her sister, Emelina, and the night of horror ending in the tragic death of eighteen-year-old Juan Miguel in Brazil.

Doris Dana felt, as did Gabriela and some others, that Yin-Yin's death was a xenophobic and senseless murder, despite the official listing of it as a suicide.

According to Miss Dana, the fierce and bitter poems that were included in *Lagar,* such as "One Word" (Una Palabra), the terrible litany of "Mourning" (Luto) and the prayerful "The Liana," (La Liana) were all expressions of Gabriela's agony and grief.

Margot Arce de Vazquez also traced the trials of travel and suffering on the part of Gabriela who, in spite of now serious illness, had summoned strength to attend the convention of writers honoring Martí in Cuba, the lectures for Responsible Freedom at Columbia University, or to carry out her duties as a member of the Committee on Women's Rights of the United Nations.

All this would leave its mark on *Wine Press,* which, according to Miss Arce, was the internalization and poetic transfiguration of these events and experiences. While the anecdotal element here is as important as in her former books, it is hidden behind a veil of hallucination and dream.

The book consists of a prologue, an epilogue, and thirteen sections. It contains no prose nor any explanatory notes such as there were in *Desolation, Tenderness,* and *Felling.*

Her poem "The Other One" serves as a prologue to the *Wine Press.*

Sections in *Wine Press* include "Fantasy" (Desvario); "War" (Guerra); "Tricks" (Jugarretas); "Mourning" (Luto); "Madwomen," (Locas Mujeres); "Nature" (Naturaleza); "Nocturnes" (Nocturnos); "Work" (Oficios); "Religious Verses" (Religiosas); "Rounds" (Rondas); "Wandering" (Vagabundje); "Time" (Tiempo); and "Earthly Message" (Recado Terrestre).

"Last Tree" (Ultimo Arbol) is the strange poem that serves as an epilogue. It sings of the definitive dream in the fresh shade of a tamarind or cedar tree, inheritor of

> What I had
> Of ash and firmament
> What I had of voice
> And what I had of silence.
>
> Sometimes I gave myself
> Solitudes given to me,
> And the tithe I paid to the lightning bolt
> Of my sweet and tremendous God.
>
> My game of give and take
> With the clouds and winds,
> And what I learned trembling,
> From secret springs.

"POEMA DE CHILE"

Gabriela's love for Chile and her remembrance of her childhood were part of her innermost being. They served as the essence of the "Poema de Chile," an extensive narrative poem that she was writing in the last years of her life. Her last work was a hymn to her country, its fruits, its forests, its mountains and seas. It was an exaltation of the country that was always present in her thoughts. She recreated from her memory each region, each animal, and each plant, right down to the last detail.

In "Poema de Chile," her spirit returns to the country, visible only to a little Indian boy of Atacama, the region where her father grew up, and a fawn that was rambling through all the regions of the country, singing of its beauties, that they could not capture. These are the northern plains, the fertile gardens of the Valley of Elqui, the farm lands of the central region, the heart of the bare forests in the extreme southern part of Chile, the rivers, the sea, and the cordilleras. They pass swiftly over the cities as Cervantes had done in Quixote, stopping to admire the natural beauty of the grass, the fruits, and the flowers.

Gabriela talks with the boy, answering his questions about the flowers and the animals of Chile and explaining to him the geography of the country. At times, the poetess speaks to the boy, at other times she talks with the fawn whose common feeling contrasts with the poetic philosophy and spirit of Gabriela.

THE PERFECTIONIST

The poetess was a perfectionist and would write about what she had observed and knew well. Gabriela had been a teacher of geography and had put together the information she had obtained about the different regions of Chile. She wrote to friends asking them for particular information about a bird or plant.

Gabriela read all the books that were published about Chile, collecting those that had illustrations about Chilean life. She always liked books that explained geography, zoology, or botany, with drawings, engravings, or photographs. In the last five years of her life, Gabriela collected books in English, French, and Spanish, with illustrations of birds, animals, and plants. They pleased her and at the same time were very useful. At times a photograph would serve her better than a thesis; a popular quatrain might be better than a story of literature.

Gabriela liked to collect figures of animals in ceramic, metal, or wood, especially those of a deer or stag.

10
The Final Years

UNIVERSAL DECLARATION FOR HUMAN RIGHTS

On the tenth of December, 1955, Gabriela was asked to take part in the United Nations celebration of the seventh anniversary of its Universal Declaration for Human Rights. She was asked to speak before the General Assembly. Dag Hammarskjöld, Secretary General of the United Nations, next to whom she was seated, paid her great honor and spoke of the debt all nations owed to her great spirit.

Gabriela had prepared a speech for the occasion, but did not deliver it because of physical weakness, exhaustion, or her habitual modesty. Her message was read to the General Assembly by a countryman who took her place, José Maza, its president.

> Eight years ago, two words went down to nations and to millions of people. They are the words we celebrate today—Human Rights.
>
> Many countries already respect human rights, but not all countries have gained them. Today, after eight years, we celebrate the birth of this movement.
>
> There are many who hesitate to grant this liberty sought by backward peoples, refusing men and women the gift so justly due them.
>
> We celebrate the anniversary of your heroic deed, but yet there remains in us a note of sadness; we look across the world and remain thoughtful.
>
> We record on this anniversary the broad and noble good

that has been achieved and wish with fervor that this date in the calendar will be absolutely glorious.

The chosen who have received this divine spark should go down to save the people that will come later.

You show them that we are full of great hope; that we do not accept living as privileged; that we continue our effort. In no sacred page is there anything that condones privilege or, at least, discrimination: two things that have cut down and offended the Son of Man.

I am very happy for your noble effort to obtain Human Rights to reach to all nations of the world. This triumph will be among the greatest that can be achieved in our epoch.[1]

MARIE-LISE GAZARIAN-GAUTIER

Marie-Lise Gazarian-Gautier was born in Paris, France, but spent many years in the United States. She received her master's and doctoral degrees at Columbia University.

Dr. Gazarian-Gautier, who had the privilege of knowing and cultivating the friendship of Gabriela Mistral in the last years of her life, wrote her doctoral thesis on Gabriela's life and work. It was later published under the title of *Gabriela Mistral, la maestra de Elqui,* by Editorial Crespillo of Buenos Aires. The translation into Spanish was made by Alberto R. Cellario.

Beginning in 1961, Dr. Gazarian-Gautier taught Spanish and Hispanic-American literature in the Department of Languages at St. John's University, in Jamaica, New York, where she was associate professor.

In 1975, the Franciscan Herald Press of Chicago published Dr. Gazarian-Gautier's *Gabriela Mistral, The Teacher from the Valley of Elqui,* the English edition of her doctoral thesis, translated by the author. The volume contained a number of photographs of Gabriela Mistral and two of Marie-Lise with her beloved friend, Gabriela.

On February 18, 1956, Gabriela was the guest of honor at a gathering of the Association of Pan-American Women in New York, giving special recognition to Chile. Dr. Gazarian-Gautier was chosen to read some of Gabriela's poems, whose thought was reflected in "La huella" (The Track), poetry that expressed her anxiety for justice, in "La cordillera," an almost humanizing description of the Andes, and in "País de la Ausencia" (Country of My Absence), which summed up memories of the countries she had known.

THE LAST YEAR

On April 15, 1956, Gabriela was able to attend a reunion of the Pan-American Union in Washington, where some of her poems were read, and on one or two occasions, she went to Princeton University to see Jaques Maritain, her old friend and spiritual brother. The great Catholic philosopher, writer, and former ambassador to the Vatican, was a visiting professor there. However, most of Gabriela's time during her final days was spent in the home of her closest friend, Doris Dana, in Roslyn Harbor. Here she was united with friends, wrote verses, and cultivated flowers in the garden, speaking with a pair of cats, a Siamese called Pussywillow ("Amente de sauce americano") and its son, Negrito, with long black hair, who was the favorite of Gabriela.

On the winter days, although she woke up at six in the morning, Gabriela stayed in bed to work. Her bedroom was transformed into a studio in which she had scattered across her bed many books and some periodicals which she read conscientiously, as if she were a student, underlining with colored pencils the passages that she felt were most important.

Meanwhile, Negrito would rest comfortably on the bed among the books, following his night of adventure in Roslyn gardens.

In this comfortable setting, Gabriela continued her writing of "Poema de Chile" and "Lagar II," correcting her writing and also making changes in poems previously published, from *Desolación* to *Lagar*.

Often times, one would find Gabriela sitting in the parlor writing verses or letters to friends, using as a table the arms of an easy chair. Her letters to friends, in reality, were interrupted conversations in which she told them of the books she was read-

The Final Years

ing, the friends she had seen, and the discussions they had maintained.

Gabriela rarely read novels, but spent most of her time with biographies, poetry, and philosophy. She often would speak of the greatness of Henri Bergson. She told Marie-Lise, "One ought to read much and especially to do it every day."

Gabriela read frequently from the Bible, underlining those passages with a colored pencil that attracted her. She liked to read over again the books she admired.

On mild days, it was pleasant for Gabriela to be seated in the garden or to pass through and water the roses and talk to them as if they were small children.

Gabriela's last public appearance was just a few weeks before her death, in 1957. It was at the Roslyn High School on Long Island, where she gave an informal talk to the American children who were learning Spanish.

FINAL ILLNESS AND DEATH

In November, 1956, Gabriela was taken for the first time to the Flower Fifth Avenue Hospital in New York City. The doctors there discovered that she was suffering from cancer, but they did not tell Doris Dana until the end of December, and they did not tell Gabriela.

During her hospital stay Dag Hammerskjöld sent her flowers. He wanted to come to see her, but the tasks of his office were too great, for in a few days he was due to travel on his ill-fated trip to the continent of Africa.

After a few days in the hospital, Gabriela returned to Roslyn. The president of Chile, Carlos Ibañez, upon learning of her sickness, wrote to her, asking if she would like to return to Chile.

A few days later, Gabriela entered the Hempstead General Hospital on Long Island. She considered it childish and a sign of weakness to be carried in on a stretcher, so she insisted on walking into the hospital. Her fortitude, despite her illness, impressed the nurses so much that one of them, a Latin-American, presented her with a large puppet that was placed on a chair near her bed.

Gabriela passed the time reading her biography, *Gabriela Mistral y el modernismo en Chile,* by Augusto Iglesias, published in Santiago in 1949. She read it as if it did not refer to herself, and that entertained her. She listened to Italian music, old songs, Hebrew-Spanish songs—"Sefardita espanola" and the "Salmos de Rey David"—and the *Cancion de Solveig* by Grieg.

Among the visitors Gabriela received were her Spanish friend Victoria Kent and the Colombian writer German Arciniegas, then a professor at Columbia University.

Victoria Ocampo, her Argentinian friend, came to visit, but was so affected on seeing the illness of the poetess that she left after staying just a few minutes.

One day when Marie-Lise was with Gabriela, Arciniegas came in accompanied by one of his daughters. The Colombian, after asking about her and about the predominant situation in Latin America, told Gabriela about the problems in Hungary, and asked if she would sign a manifesto defending the Hungarian Revolution. Gabriela signed without hesitation.

Due to the severity of her illness, Gabriela remained at the hospital; nevertheless, at times, she acted like a hostess, attentive and generous, forgetting that she was in the hospital. She would bestow attention on her guests and offer regrets, with a bit of coquetry, that she had to receive them in bed. She maintained her good humor and said that the room she was occupying in the hospital had been made for a millionaire.

As her condition seemed to improve, Gabriela returned to the home of Doris Dana. On one of her better days, she received a visit from Jacques Maritain. They spoke much of God, of life and death, and of religious themes, which were so near to them both.

Soon afterward, Gabriela suffered a severe hemorrhage and was taken again to the Hempstead General Hospital at the direction of her doctor, Martin Goldfarb, on December 19, 1956. This time, she was placed in a private room on the fourth floor. Here, she could see the great trees covered with snow.

When Marie-Lise came to see her one day, Gabriela, who

The Final Years

was seated on the bed, placed her visitor's hand beween hers. Upon a table at her side was a picture of her mother that she always carried with her and the crucifix that she had brought along. She spoke of her mother as if she were already united with her in spirit. She seemed to be far away, near to her mother and those she loved. From the window they viewed a beautiful sunset. When the sun went down at nightfall, she took the other hand of Marie-Lise and told her, with a warm and human smile, "We will see Tuesday. I know, nevertheless, that I am going to die. I know that I suffer from heart disease and from diabetes."

On the second of January, in 1957, Gabriela asked for her final communion. Twenty-four hours later, she fell into a coma and never regained consciousness. The Chilean Jesuit priest Renalto Poblata, of Santiago, gave her the papal benediction.

Gabriela died on January 10, 1957, at 4:18 A.M. after a hard struggle. She died of cancer of the pancreas. Her doctors were Alfred Vogl, Martin Goldfarb, and Blas Bellolio, also a Chilean.

Gabriela finally reached the peace that she had so much desired. She had searched for truth and it had become a part of her.

Many people, humble and powerful, assisted in the funeral services in New York for Gabriela Mistral, Among them was Robert Wagner, the mayor, diplomatic representatives of the American republics and Spain, and many friends.

On Saturday, January 14, 1957, at ten in the morning, Cardinal Francis Spellman held a funeral mass for Gabriela in the St. Patrick's Cathedral. After the service, the coffin was escorted to the airport and placed on a plane destined for Lima. In the Peruvian capital, it was transferred to a Chilean plane and taken to Gabriela's native country on January 19, 1957.

Speaking of her good friend, Doris Dana told Marie-Lise, "Gabriela taught us a lesson; through working and learning and explaining life, she gave us strength."

Marie-Lise summed up her own feelings:

> I, who had been so near to her, knew that she was not here, that her frail and inert body was only a covering which had

contained her soul. This could not be Gabriela, because she was real, a part of the same life. Her penetrating green eyes, her warm, almost childlike smile, full of mischief, was now in our hearts.

She had expressed in her work the need of leaving her body to dissolve in nature, had arrived at only a spirit free of all human limitations. Her universe had no frontiers; in her frank love of nature, she had embraced all humanity in order to form a great country. From childhood, she had been interested in astronomy, in learning that there was more than our world, that world which was not enough. She had found God, and life in him was more, and now she was face to face with Him. The tired body was ready to be carried to its resting place that was its destiny, the Andes Mountains, among her beloved people in Monte Grande.[2]

OBSERVANCE IN CHILE

The president of Chile, General Carlos Ibañez, stated, "Her death represents an irreplaceable spiritual loss to our country and its contemporary literature." Then he decreed three days of national mourning. All official buildings as well as schools were closed. The tricolored flag was lowered to half-mast.

Accompanying the coffin to the Central House of the University of Chile was an escort including ministers of state, members of Congress, members of the diplomatic corps, intellectuals, students, workers, and people of all social classes who loved, admired, and respected Gabriela Mistral.

The rector of the institution received the coffin in the salon of honor. Four hundred children of *Liceo Number Six* (of which Gabriela was the first director), formed the honor guard. The choirs sang, "Go, sweet death," by Johann Sebastian Bach. More than two thousand persons paid homage.

Services were completed in the General Cemetery of Santiago, where the remains were deposited in niche number ninety-seven of the mausoleum reserved for members of the Society of Primary Education, until it was transferred to Monte Grande.

On the monument of granite was engraved a fragment of the poem "Teacher's Prayer":

The Final Years

> Lord, you who taught,
> Pardon me, that I also teach.

In the interior of the niche was placed a parchment with the complete poem of "La Oración" along with a bust of the poetess by Laura Rodig.

UNIVERSAL RECOGNITION

All Latin American and many European countries paid homage to the Chilean poetess-teacher. Israel, which did not grant titles or medals to individuals, gave her name to a vast forest zone with thirty-five thousand trees.

In Chile, a complete number of *Anales* of the University was dedicated to her. It contained articles and portions of books written about her and also some of her work.

The same year of her death, the Editorial Zig Zag of Santiago also published an anthology of her works. Many countries printed commemorative stamps.

The name of Gabriela Mistral had the same force as the "mistral" wind. Schools, libraries, and cultural centers were named for her. As far back as 1945, schools had been named for her, including two in Argentina, two in Chile, two in Colombia, three in Ecuador, one in Guatemala, one in El Salvador, and two in Mexico. Her name was placed on a library in Vicuña, as well as in Mexico. Busts and statues were dedicated to her in many countries. In October, 1959, a Chilean painter exhibited in her memory his paintings of the poetess at the University of Chile.

The chief of the delegation from Chile to the United Nations, Robert Aldulante, said:

> Gabriela has sounded through the world an expression of spiritual comprehension of deep spiritual tones. From wherever she was—in conferences, in literary discussions, in reunions of students, in a universal tribunal, or in the court of the United Nations—she poured out generously her feeling

for all mentalities and this suppression of limiting all passions to arrive at a universalism that permits us to understand each other.[3]

A full page in the *New York Times Book Review* was dedicated to Gabriela's memory. Mildred Adams wrote:

> Gabriela's clarity and precision, her passion and that characteristic which can only be called her nobility of soul are acceptable as ideals. She will not quickly vanish from the literary consciousness of those who value the Spanish tongue.[4]

In the Spanish language *El Diario de Nueva York,* Ramon Sender declared:

> There are some poets who hide behind their verses. Others give themselves freely from their first poem, and so it was with Gabriela Mistral.[5]

On January 10, 1957, the General Assembly of the United Nations interrupted the debate on Hungary to pay tribute to the memory of the Chilean poetess.

Through many years, Gabriela was a frequent contributor to many periodicals in South America, Mexico, Europe, and the United States. In addition to her poetry, she wrote articles on sociological, educational, and cultural subjects. Her poems have been translated into French, German, Swedish, Italian, and English.

Among those who have translated her work into English in various periodicals and anthologies are Alice Stone Blackwell, Katherine Chapin, Dorothy Conzelman, H. R. Hayes, Isabel K. McDermott, Muna Lee de Muñoz, Donald Devenish, and Thomas Walsh.

As was noted earlier, a Spanish biographical study, *Gabriela Mistral, la maestra de Elqui,* written by Marie-Lise Gazarian-Gautier as a doctoral thesis and published by Editorial Crespillo in Buenos Aires appeared in 1973, and a translation into English by the author was published in 1975 by the *Franciscan Herald Press* of

The Final Years

Chicago under the title of *Gabriela Mistral, The Teacher from the Valley of Elqui.*

Although Gabriela had been awarded the Nobel Prize for Literature in 1945, no collection of Spanish poems translated into English had yet appeared in book form in 1956, except in anthologies, the most extensive of which had appeared in a volume by Alice Stone Blackwell in 1930. Following Gabriela's death in 1957, Bernard Perry of the Indiana University Press requested that Langston Hughes translate some of her poems into English. The result was *Selected Poems of Gabriela Mistral,* translated into English with an introduction by Langston Hughes, published in a hard-bound edition in 1957. It was released as a paperback in 1965.

A second volume, also entitled *Selected Poems of Gabriela Mistral,* was translated and edited by Doris Dana. It contained an introduction by Margaret Bates. It was published by the Johns Hopkins Press of Baltimore, Maryland, in 1971.

The Spanish edition of *Poesias Completas de Gabriela Mistral,* prepared by Margaret Bates, was published in Madrid in 1970. It contained the poems from *Desolación, Ternura, Tala* and *Lagar,* with an introduction by Esther de Caceros.

Some of Gabriela's experiences in Mexico in 1922-1924 were included in *Lecturas Para Mujeres,* which was first published in Mexico. Another edition published in 1967 contains an introduction by Palma Guillén written on July 1, 1966. A third edition was published by the Editorial Porrua, S.A. Argentina 15, Mexico 1, D.F. in 1971.

The income from the sale of publications from Latin America was left to Doris Dana and Gabriela's Mexican friend, Palma Guillén de Nicolau d'Olivir. Palma declined the legacy on behalf of the poor children of Chile. Doris Dana remained the only heir of Gabriela and her literary executor. The poetess left to Chile her gold medal and the Nobel Prize.

As a tribute and according to Gabriela's desire to help young writers, the municipality of Santiago sponsored a literary contest of novels, essays, and poetry called Concurso Literario Gabriela **Mistral.**

In her testament, Gabriela expressed her wish to be interred in Monte Grande, the humble village of her childhood, in the interior of the province of Coquimbo, surrounded by green hills. Because of her love for the people, Gabriela asked that the income from her books published in Latin America be remitted to the Franciscan Order for distribution among the poor children of Monte Grande.

It was not until 1960, three years after her death, that Gabriela's remains were finally removed to Monte Grande, the village of her childhood. The people of Chile paid tribute to their spiritual mother in a moving ceremony. Doris Dana came to Santiago as a guest of the government to take part in the ceremonies.

DORIS DANA'S MISSION

The next year, in 1961, Doris Dana was sent to Latin America by the U.S. Department of State to preside over conferences on her friend Gabriela Mistral. In her journey which began on the thirteenth of April, she visited twelve countries—Puerto Rico, Mexico, Guatemala, El Salvador, Honduras, Jamaica, Colombia, Ecuador, Peru, Argentina, Chile, and Venezuela—and held eighty-six conferences in forty cities.

With photographs, films, and magnetic disks, she helped to revive the familiar figure of Gabriela. Doris carried with her disks recorded by the poetess. Through them, Gabriela spoke to the public in her own voice—conversations, the monologue about the poetry of Unamuno and of de Antero de Quental, and so on.

In Chile, Doris distributed among the children copies of the book of *Gabriela's Poesia Completas,* published in Spain in 1958 by the Editorial Aguilar. In the name of Gabriela, she distributed both books and warm clothing in different parts of the country.

Epilogue

Nothing could better express the constant love of the poetess for her country than her "Poema de Chile." In this extensive narrative poem, Gabriela imagines that after death she will return to her country as a phantom, or spirit, and ramble through all its territories, explaining in detail the beauties of the land.

Early in life Gabriela had expressed her creed:

> My own small literary work is a little Chilean for its sobriety and its roughness. That was done in teaching and living among my children. I came from the country and I am one of them. My great loves are my faith, the country, and the poetry.

Gabriela wrote, "You shall love beauty, for it is the shadow of God over the universe."

Gabriela's conception of beauty and its meaning for both the artist, the teacher, and the lay person are revealed in her "Decalogue of the Artist," which appears earlier in this volume.

Gabriela considered her most important post to be that of a country schoolteacher. She felt that the mission of the teacher should be that of an artist, as she would strive to create beauty and the love for God's creation in the minds and souls of those she taught. Let us look again at that portion of her "Teacher's Prayer," which I have translated from the Spanish into English:

> Let me be more mother than the mother herself in my love and defense of the child who is not flesh of my flesh. Help me to make one of my children my most perfect poem, and leave within him or her my most melodious melody from that day when my own lips no longer sing.

Notes

Chapter 1

1. Marie-Lise Gazarian-Gautier, *La maestra de Elqui* (Buenos Aires: Editorial Crespillo, 1973), translated from the Spanish by the author.

Chapter 2

1. Gazarian-Gautier, *La maestra de Elqui*, p. 35.
2. *Ibid.*, p. 35.
3. *Ibid.*, p. 36.
4. *Ibid.*
5. *Ibid.*, p. 37.

Chapter 3

1. Marie-Lise Gazarian-Gautier, *The Teacher from the Valley of Elqui* (Chicago: Francisco Herald Press, 1975), p. 23.
2. *Ibid.*
3. *Ibid.*
4. *Ibid.*
5. *Ibid.*, p. 24.
6. *Ibid.*
7. *Ibid.*
8. *Ibid.*
9. *Ibid.*, p. 25.
10. *Ibid.*, p. 26.

Chapter 4

1. Gazarian-Gautier, *The Teacher from the Valley of Elqui, op. cit.*, p. 27.
2. *Ibid.*
3. Gazarian-Gautier, *La maestra de Elqui, op. cit.*, p. 50.

4. *Ibid.*
5. *Ibid.,* p. 51.
6. *Ibid.,* p. 52.
7. *Ibid.*

Chapter 5

1. Palma Guillén de Nicolau, *Gabriela Mistral (1922-1924)* in *Lecturas para mujeres,* Third Edition (Mexico: Editorial Porrua, 1971), p. ix.
2. *Ibid.*
3. *Ibid.,* p. vii.
4. *Ibid.,* p. viii.
5. *Ibid.*
6. Doria Dana, *Selected Poems of Gabriela Mistral* (Baltimore: John Hopkins Press, 1971), p. xxv.
7. Committee on Cooperation in Latin America, *Report for 1921,* edited by Samuel Guy Inman (New York: CCLA, 1921), p. 3.
8. Guillén, *op. cit.,* p. xi.
9. *Ibid.,* p. xii.
10. *Ibid.*
11. *Ibid.*

Chapter 6

1. Margot de Arce Vasquez, *The Poet and Her Work* (New York: New York University Press, 1944), p. 141.
2. *Ibid.*
3. *Ibid.,* p. 44.
4. Dana, *op. cit.,* p. 49.
5. *Ibid.,* p. 41.
6. *Ibid.,* p. 40.
7. Samuel Guy Inman, *Ventures in Inter-American Friendship* (New York: Missionary Education Movement in the United States and Canada, 1929), p. 8.
8. *Ibid.,* p. 9.
9. *Ibid.,* pp. 62-63.
10. *Ibid.,* p. 63.
11. *Ibid.*
12. *Ibid.,* pp. 62-63.
13. Samuel Guy Inman, ed., *Christian Work in Latin America,* vol. 1 (New York: Fleming H. Revell Company, 1925), p. 341.
14. *Ibid.,* p. 342.

15. *Ibid.*
16. *Ibid.*, pp. 342, 343.
17. *Ibid.*, p. 343.
18. Gazarian-Gautier, *La maestra de Elqui, op. cit.*, p. 68.

Chapter 7

1. Gazarian-Gautier, *La maestra de Elqui, op. cit.*, pp. 68-69.
2. *Ibid.*, p. 75.
3. *Ibid.*, p. 82.
4. *Ibid.*, p. 85.
5. Arce, *op. cit.*, p. 48.

Chapter 8

1. Gazarian-Gautier, *La maestra de Elqui, op. cit.*, pp. 92-93.
2. *Ibid.*, p. 102.
3. Gazarian-Gautier, *The Teacher from the Valley of Elqui, op. cit.*, p. 81.
4. *Ibid.*, p. 82.
5. *Ibid.*
6. *Ibid.*
7. *Ibid.*
8. Langston Hughes, *Selected Poems of Gabriela Mistral* (Bloomington; Indiana University Press, 1957), p. 15.
9. *Ibid.*, p. 16.
10. Gazarian-Gautier, *The Teacher from the Valley of Elqui, op. cit.*, p. 83.

Chapter 9

1. Gazarian-Gautier, *La maestra de Elqui, op. cit.* pp. 112, 113.
2. Gazarian-Gautier, *The Teacher from the Valley of Elqui, op. cit.*, p. 86.
3. *Ibid.*, p. 96.
4. *Ibid.*

Chapter 10

1. Gazarian-Gautier, *The Teacher from the Valley of Elqui, op. cit.*, p. 101.
2. Gazarian-Gautier, *La maestra de Elqui, op. cit.*, p. 135.
3. *Ibid.*
4. Hughes, *op. cit.*, p. 12.
5. *Ibid.*

Bibliography

SELECTED WORKS OF GABRIELA MISTRAL

Poesía

Desolación. First edition. New York: New York Instituto de las Espanas, 1922, 248 pp. Second edition. Santiago: Nasciento, 1923, 357 pp., Santiago: Nasciento, 1926, 342 pp.
Lagar. Santiago: Ed. del Pacifico, 1954. 188 pp. (Sus Obras Selectas. Vol. 6)
Poesias Completas: Desolación/Ternura/Tala/Lagar I. Ediciones definitiva, autorizado, preparado por Margaret Bates, Con una introducción por Esther Caceres. Madrid, Spain, Aguilar. c. Doris Dana, 1964, Cuarto edition, 1968. Primera reimpression, 1970. 836 pp.
Tala; poemas. Buenos Aires: Sur, 1938, 386 pp.
Tala; poemas. Buenos Aires: Losada, 1946, 163 pp.
Ternura, canciones de niños. Montevideo: Garcia, 1924.
Ternura. Madrid: Edit. Santurnino Calleja, 1924, 108 pp.

Prosa

Lecturas para mujeres. Mexico, D.F.: Secretaria de Educación, 1923, 395 pp.
Lecturas para mujeres destinados a la del languajo. Mexico, 1924; Madrid: Tip Moderna, 1924, 450 pp.
Lecturas para mujeres (Gabriela Mistral, 1922-1924), Por Palma Guillén. Third edition. Mexico: Editorial Porrua, S.A., 1971, 267 pp.

Texts in Spanish and English

Blackwell, Alice Stone. *Some Spanish American Poets*. New York, London: D. Appleton & Co., 1930.

Dana, Doris. *Selected Poems of Gabriela Mistral*. A bilingual edition translated and edited by Doris Dana, with an introduction by Margaret Bates. Baltimore: Johns Hopkins Press, 1971, 235 pp.

Critical and Biographical Studies of Gabriela Mistral in Spanish and/or in English

Arce, de Vasquez, Margot. "*Vida y poesia de Gabriela Mistral.*" *Asomante* (San Juan, Puerto Rico), April-June, 1946.

_____. *The Poet and Her Work*. Translated by Helen Masslo Anderson. New York: New York University Press, 1964, 158 pp.

Figueroa, Virgilio. *La divina Gabriela*. Santiago de Chile: Imp. El Esuergo, 1933, 318 pp.

Hughes, Langston. *Selected Poems of Gabriela Mistral*, with an introduction and translations by Langston Hughes. Bloomington, Indiana: Indiana University Press, 1937, 119 pp.

Inman, Samuel Guy. *Ventures in Inter-American Friendship*. New York: Missionary Education Movement of the United States and Canada, 144 pp.

Gazarian-Gautier, Marie-Lise. *Gabriela Mistral: La maestra de Elqui*. (Version Espanola de Alberto R. Cellario) Buenos Aires: Editorial Crespillo, 1973, paperback, 148 pp. Gabriela Mistral: *The Teacher from the Valley of Elqui*. English translation from the Spanish by the author. Chicago: Franciscan Herald Press 1975, 168 pp., with photos.

Rudd, Margaret T. *The Lone Heretic, A Biography of Miguel de Unamuno*. Austin: Texas University Press, 1963, reprinted by Gordian Press, Inc. New York.

_____. *Gabriela Mistral*. A biography in progress, as yet unpublished.

Taylor, Martin C. *Gabriela Mistral's Religious Sensibility*. Berkeley and Los Angeles: University of California Press, 1968, 191 pp.